G

IS

LING!

TO MY PARENTS,

ÖZGÜL + MAHMUT,

WHO MADE ME

TO MY KIDS,

AWA + ALEV,

WHO TRANSFORMED ME

design the
LONG
LIFE
you love

A STEP-BY-STEP GUIDE TO
LOVE, PURPOSE, WELL-BEING,
AND FRIENDSHIP

ayse birsel

Running Press

PHILADELPHIA

ARE YOU INTERESTED IN

THINKING LIKE A DESIGNER?

IF SO, THIS BOOK IS FOR YOU—

NO MATTER YOUR AGE.

IT'S INSPIRED BY THE LESSONS

I LEARNED FROM PEOPLE WHO

ARE PIONEERS OF LONG LIFE.

SOLVE FOR LONG LIFE
SOLVE FOR ALL AGES

LOVE

PURPOSE

WELL-BEING

FRIENDSHIP

CONTENTS

A LONG LIFE

The other night, my teenage daughter said to me, "You have another forty to fifty years to live, Mom—as much as you've already lived. This is very exciting!"

Thinking about a long life is very exciting indeed. It's also a new phenomenon. Fifty years ago, people rarely lived past their sixties. Living into one's seventies was considered the mark of a long life. Today, seventy feels young, eighty feels normal, and ninety is within reach.

This changes everything for all of us. Boomers, Gen Xers, millennials, postmillennials. If we are the first people to have a lot more time on this planet, how do we want to live those extra years? Who do we want to be now? What do we want going forward? What brings us joy? What is the purpose of our lives?

This new horizon of life is as important and exciting as the invention of moving pictures. Or that of automobiles, or even space travel. My point is, when a change this big happens, innovation follows.

When it comes to our lives, we are our own innovators—so let's begin to learn how to do just that. Welcome to *Design the Long Life You Love!*

You deserve an original life, and now more than ever, you have the chance to imagine it. Let's start!

PART 0.0

THINKING
LIKE A
DESIGNER

DESIGNING YOUR LIFE

It all began with a simple idea. I believe life is our biggest project. And as a designer, I decided to test this idea by applying my design thinking process, Deconstruction:Reconstruction, to my life. From this idea, I began Design the Life You Love as an experiment in 2010.

I was my first test subject. I created exercises and tried them out. Then I tried them on my friends. My friends told their friends, and the whole thing grew by word of mouth—suddenly, lots of people were designing the lives they loved. Linda Tischler, the senior design editor of *Fast Company* at that time, wrote about

my method in *Huffington Post*. She called the piece "Forget New Year's Resolutions. This Year, Use Design Tools to Redesign Your Life," and that put the idea on the map.

MAURO PORCINI, CHIEF DESIGN OFFICER OF PEPSICO, NICKNAMED ME THE "DESIGN EVANGELISTA" BECAUSE I TEACH PEOPLE THE WORLD OVER HOW TO THINK LIKE A DESIGNER USING OUR SHARED PROJECT—OUR LIVES.

As a designer, I've created many things in my life. No one has ever written to me to say, "Your potato peeler for Target changed my life," or "Your office system for Herman Miller changed my life." But they do tell me that designing their life in this way has been transformative. That feedback is why I love teaching people how to design their lives.

TRANSFORMING YOUR LIFE BY DESIGN

13 design the

Welcome to the global, multicultural, multigenerational community of people who believe our lives are our biggest project. Thousands of people across the globe have designed and redesigned their lives using my books and design process.

90

life you love

The most important thing I have learned—from people ages thirteen to ninety-plus—is that humans are extraordinarily creative. You don't need to be a designer to design your life. You just need to think like a designer. All *you* need is a design process and tools. Just like me.

WHAT IS DESIGN?

This is a book about thinking like a designer. So what, exactly, does thinking like a designer mean? The *Oxford English Dictionary* defines *design* as "A plan or drawing produced to show the look and function or workings of a building, garment, or other object before it is built or made."

When you look at the etymology of *design*, you'll find that it comes from planning something in your mind and drawing a map of that plan.

The book you are holding is about both planning your life—in this case, your long life—and drawing a map for it.

design:
PLAN (MIND) + DRAW (BODY)

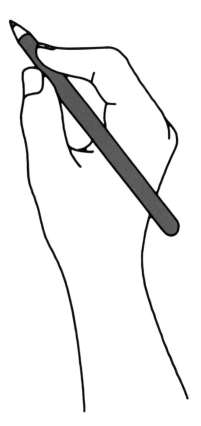

FOR ME, DESIGN IS IMAGINING
THE FUTURE YOU LOVE BASED
ON WHAT YOU KNOW TODAY.

TOOLS
OF DESIGN

Cognitive science tells us there is a direct correlation between the brain and the hand. To imagine, use your pen. In fact, all you need to design the long life you love is this book and your favorite pen.

DESIGNING YOUR LIFE IS YOGA FOR THE MIND

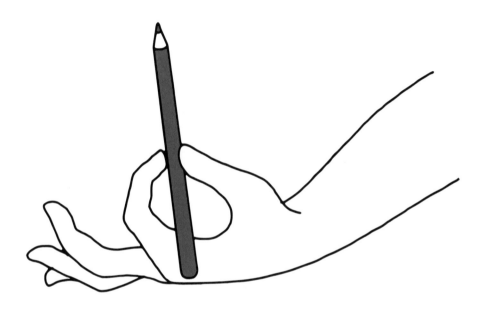

Now that you know the connection between your brain and your hand, you can understand why my friend Jack Gelman calls my process *yoga for the mind*. Design is the perfect mind and body activity.

MY PROCESS

1. DECONSTRUCT

2. EXPLORE

Deconstruction:Reconstruction (DE:RE) is my design thinking process. It comes from my expertise of designing products, including ones you have probably used, held, or sat on, like a toilet seat for TOTO, an office system for Herman Miller, kitchen

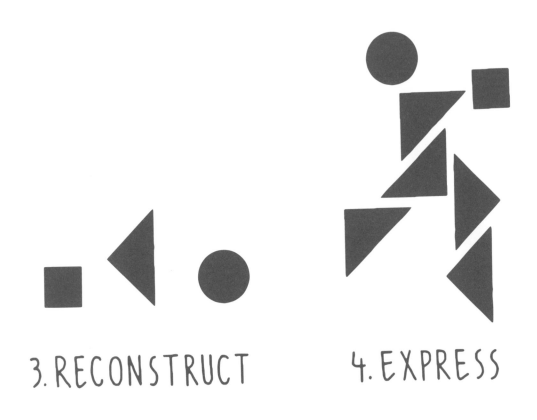

3. RECONSTRUCT

4. EXPRESS

utensils for Target, and concept cars for Toyota. It is also the process my team and I use to codesign with our clients to bring new solutions to old problems. In this book, I will show you how you can use this same process to design your long life.

THINKING LIKE A DESIGNER

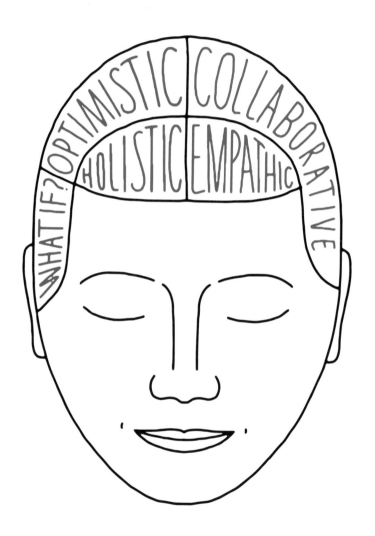

Are you optimistic? Do you have empathy for other people? Do you like having a bird's-eye view of things? Do you often use the words *what if*? Do you enjoy collaborating with others?

If so, you're already thinking like a designer. Optimism—the belief that we will find a better solution no matter how hard the problem—fuels our energy, calms our fears, and propels us forward.

We put ourselves in other people's shoes to understand what they need and want. A designer's empathy is human-centered. We think holistically in order to see the big picture, read the patterns, and connect the dots in new and different ways.

We ask questions, knowing our answers often come from unexpected, counter-intuitive places.

THESE PRINCIPLES ARE THE FOUNDATION OF MY THINKING AND OF THIS BOOK.

And we love to collaborate so that we can learn from each other, to inspire and build on each other's ideas.

PLAYFUL

When we're playing, we're like kids—unafraid to make mistakes. We learn by doing. Some of what we try works, and some of it doesn't. Even when something fails, we learn what we need to make it work the next time. This is why being playful is the mood of design.

It's counterintuitive, but the more serious or complex the challenge, the more playful we become as designers. We need to play with ideas until we have one that captures our imagination.

THIS RABBIT IS YOUR
REMINDER TO BE PLAYFUL
WHEN YOU DESIGN.

SIMPLICITY
BEYOND
COMPLEXITY

SIMPLICITY

"Less is more." This aphorism, attributed to the architect-designer Ludwig Mies van der Rohe, is my compass as a designer.

When I get lost in the messy middle, I look for my creative North Star—less is more.

Less is more is about finding simplicity beyond complexity. It is making more with fewer parts. It is eliminating what is not needed to make space for what matters. It is about trusting the process enough to hang in when creativity gets weird and messy (and it always does), so you can arrive at elegant solutions on the other side.

It is the same here. I want to help you find simplicity beyond the complexity of life, the only way I know how—through design.

PART 1.0

A
LONGER
LIFE

THERE COMES A TIME WHEN YOU
HAVE DONE THE THINGS LIFE EXPECTS
OF *YOU*—SCHOOL, WORK, FAMILY.
THAT'S WHEN YOU'RE READY TO
EXPLORE WHAT *YOU* EXPECT OF LIFE.
MOST OF US EXPERIENCE THIS STAGE
IN OUR FORTIES AND FIFTIES, BUT
FOR YOU, IT MIGHT COME EARLIER
OR LATER. WHENEVER IT HAPPENS,
IT'S A GREAT TIME FOR DESIGNING
YOUR LIFE.

WHAT LIFE EXPECTS of YOU

WHAT YOU EXPECT of LIFE

50+

Codesign

My biggest takeaway from a decade of practicing Design the Life You Love is this: people are extraordinarily creative, even if they're not trained as designers. And if they can design their lives—our biggest and most complex project—they can design anything that is a subset of life.

With this idea in mind, my team and I developed codesign as an integral part of the design practice in our New York–based innovation studio. We now codesign every project, from luxury vehicles to laundry experiences to women's health, with users like you.

Codesign, or co-creation, is about including users or customers as partners in the creative process. It helps us understand users not only through observation and interviews but also through mutual creativity and collaboration. This is exactly how we did our research on aging, which upended all of our old preconceptions (and led to the book you're holding right now!).

CODESIGN

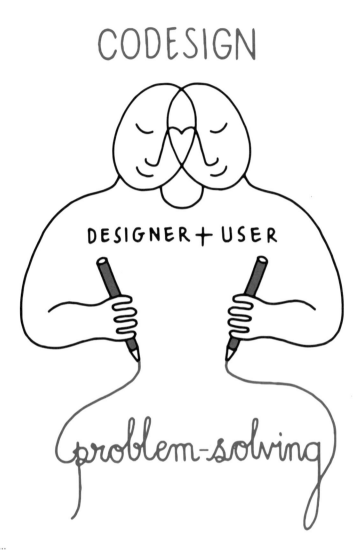

DESIGNER + USER

problem-solving

QUOTE FROM *INCUMBENTS STRIKE BACK, INSIGHTS FROM THE GLOBAL C-SUITE STUDY*, IBM INSTITUTE FOR BUSINESS VALUE.

"Robust co-creation communities empower people so that trust flourishes. Intimacy leads to a better understanding of human motivations; a key goal of design thinking is to gain customer empathy."

DESIGN THE AGING YOU LOVE

My team and I became interested in older people as our parents started aging. We were three women collaborators—Leah Caplan, Seda Evis, and me—sandwiched between our older parents and our younger kids. By observing them, we realized that while the market was overflowing with design for kids, there was little good design for our parents. We decided to do our own research and see if anyone else was interested in the aging space.

Ana Pinto da Silva at Amazon became our first client. Together, we collaborated on the first Design the Life You Love sixty-five-plus codesign project. Then Bruce Chernof, president of The SCAN Foundation (TSF), asked us to be their innovation partners.

ANA PINTO DA SILVA   BRUCE CHERNOF

Together, we invited older people to come and be a designer with us for a day. For one year, we traveled across the US—east, west, north, and south, in urban, suburban, and rural areas—and asked people who were sixty-five-plus to design their lives with us.

Our learnings from these two codesign projects with older adults inform the insights in this book.

THE PROJECTS WITH ANA AND BRUCE TRANSFORMED OUR UNDERSTANDING OF OLDER PEOPLE—THESE WISE INDIVIDUALS WHO HAVE LIVED THE LONGEST.

"THE SCAN FOUNDATION IS AN INDEPENDENT PUBLIC CHARITY DEVOTED TO TRANSFORMING CARE FOR OLDER ADULTS IN WAYS THAT PRESERVE DIGNITY AND ENCOURAGE INDEPENDENCE."

SETTING THE STAGE: SUMMER OF 2019

SEZER · İSMET · MAMADOU

AYŞE · GÜN · MAHMUT

ÖZGÜL · ESİN · ALEV

ÜNER · GISELE

MY ELDERS

I am a New Yorker now, but I grew up in Turkey, and every summer, I go to the Aegean Sea to work and be close to my parents. The summer of 2019 was no different. John Zapolski, a serial entrepreneur who also had taken a keen interest in aging, had become the VP of innovation at TSF, and I were collaborating virtually on our research, he in LA and I in Çeşme.

As I was drawing and mapping my insights and sharing them with John, I was surrounded by my aunts and uncles in their seventies and eighties. We would swim, have teas, and eat dinners together. On more than one occasion, John had to wait patiently while I addressed a knock on my window from an uncle or aunt heading to or from the beach, explaining to them that I was in a client meeting. (This would make John and me laugh.) Serendipitously, I was bathed not just in the Aegean but also in this day-to-day living with older folks.

Everything I experienced that summer somehow found its way to my understanding of a long life. That summer of 2019 was joyful and transformative.

LOVE YOUR ELDERS

I come from a culture that reveres its elders. My mother would make sure I visited my great-uncle, Münir Birsel, every week when I was a kid. I complained every time. One day, my uncle said to me, "Ayse, be independent and learn to stand on your own two feet. Don't depend on anyone." I never forgot his advice. He was in his eighties, and I was twelve. Another time my aunt Alev told me to not feel guilty about moving to New York, which liberated me and allowed me to live my own life. To this day, my uncle Gün advises me when I have a knotty problem.

CHRISTINE DOWNTON

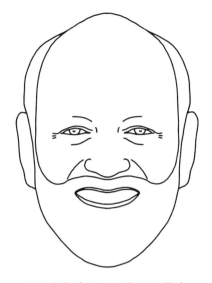

MARSHALL GOLDSMITH

WHAT I KNEW INTUITIVELY WHEN I WAS 20, I KNOW FOR A FACT IN MY 50S. WE HAVE SO MUCH TO LEARN FROM OLDER PEOPLE. CODESIGNING LIFE WITH THEM ONLY STRENGTHENED THIS BELIEF. THIS BOOK IS INSPIRED BY LESSONS I LEARNED FROM OLDER PEOPLE, LESSONS WE CAN USE AT ANY AGE, THE YOUNGER THE BETTER.

I came of age in New York, a culture that adores its youth. But even in New York, my Turkish admiration for elders didn't wane. My teacher and first friend in New York City, Rowena Reed Kostellow, was eighty-plus years old when I met her at Pratt Institute. I have been emulating her ever since. Ralph Caplan, the author of *By Design*, was instrumental in my career and acted as my mentor until he died at age ninety-five and a half. Christine Downton, who invented one of the first financial apps in the world, is my role model for being ageless. Marshall Goldsmith, author of *What Got You Here Won't Get You There*, is my mentor and coach, and I am his. We constantly debate who changed whose life.

ASTRONAUTS OF LIFE

One of the reasons older people are a gold mine of inspiration when designing your life is because the stage of life they're currently in didn't exist before. Older people are like astronauts of life—a term Seda Evis coined during our research—going where no one has gone before.

As we all aspire to live a long life, we can learn so much from these life astronauts. These are people with incredible endurance, vigorous training, and loads of courage who are exploring this new time that has opened up due to advances in health care and relative peace in many parts of the world.

We can learn so much from these astronauts, like seeing the beauty in small things, starting something new, and accepting change and going with it, undeterred and crystal clear about the things that matter.

Episode

LONG LIFE

VIII

ASTRONAUTS

PART 2.0

WHAT'S GREAT ABOUT A LONG LIFE?

ABOUT
THIS BOOK

THIS BOOK IS FOR EVERYONE WHO IS

INTERESTED IN DEFINING THEIR LONG

LIFE, USING DESIGN THINKING TOOLS.

IT'S AN INTERACTIVE BOOK WITH

EXERCISES THAT WILL HELP YOU THINK

CREATIVELY BY ASKING YOU TO VISUALIZE

YOUR LIFE. IT IS FULL OF INSIGHTS I HAVE

LEARNED FROM WISE PEOPLE WHO HAVE

LIVED THE LONGEST. IT IS ORGANIZED INTO

THE FOUR THEMES OF LOVE, PURPOSE,

WELL-BEING, AND FRIENDSHIP.

USE THESE INSIGHTS TO LOVE BETTER,

TO FIND PURPOSE, TO PRACTICE WELL-BEING, AND TO MAKE FRIENDS. IF YOU'RE IN YOUR TWENTIES AND THIRTIES, OPEN THIS BOOK AND YOUR HEART TO ALL THE THINGS YOU CAN LEARN NOW, WITHOUT WAITING TO BE OLDER. IF YOU'RE IN YOUR FORTIES AND FIFTIES, OPEN THIS BOOK TO DESIGN YOUR LIFE, BUT ALSO TO HAVE EMPATHY FOR YOUR AGING PARENTS, COLLEAGUES, AND FRIENDS. AND IF YOU'RE IN YOUR SIXTIES, SEVENTIES, EIGHTIES, AND NINETIES, OPEN THIS BOOK TO DESIGN AND REDESIGN YOUR LIFE. YOU ARE THE EXPERT AT LIFE, AND WE ARE ALL LEARNING FROM YOU.

EXPANSIONIST
POINT OF VIEW

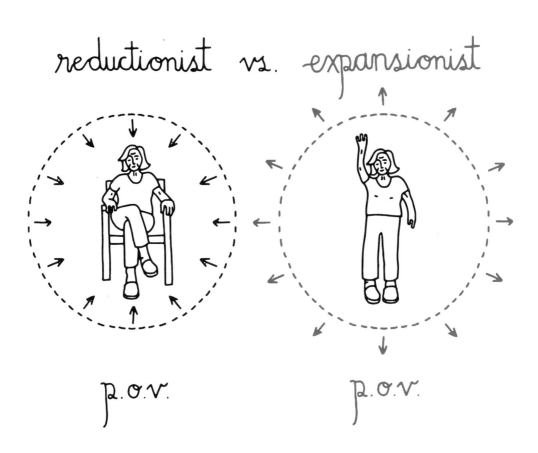

reductionist vs. expansionist

p.o.v.

p.o.v.

One of the participants in our codesign sessions said, "Be an optimist. Yes, I fell. Yes, I had a scrape. But I didn't break anything." Most of the research on aging reduces older people to the sum of the changes happening in their lives as they age.

What motivated me to write this book is an alternative, expansionist point of view that we learned from codesigning with older adults. None of the participants would dispute the difficulties and challenges related to health, family, finances, and social life inherent in living longer. But they wouldn't accept a reductionist point of view as being representative of who they are either. They would find it old-fashioned.

WE FOUND OLDER PEOPLE HAVE A GROWTH MINDSET. ON THE ONE HAND, THEY'RE MASTERS WHO BELIEVE IN THEIR TALENTS AND EXPERTISE. ON THE OTHER HAND, THEY HAVE THE BEGINNER'S MIND AND ARE INTERESTED IN LEARNING AND EXPANDING THEIR EXPERIENCES.

People today are much more optimistic about living long lives. They don't see their lives as shrinking. Instead, they see their lives as expanding and growing.

Their optimism permeates this book on every page. According to the very people who are leading long lives, living longer is thrilling.

OLDER ADULTHOOD IS THRILLING

is ON!

This is the moment when you have a lifetime of experience and, hopefully, some self-awareness, some disposable income, and some free time to do what *you* want.

MASTER OF
YOUR LIFE

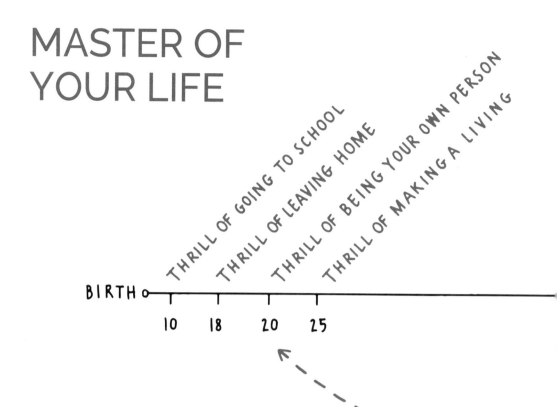

THRILL OF GOING TO SCHOOL

THRILL OF LEAVING HOME

THRILL OF BEING YOUR OWN PERSON

THRILL OF MAKING A LIVING

BIRTH

10   18   20   25

There are two time periods when we feel like the masters of our lives. The first time is around eighteen, when many people leave home for the first time. The second time is around sixty, when your kids might be leaving home or you might be leaving work.

Part of what makes longer life thrilling is the opportunity to reclaim your time to make what you want out of it.

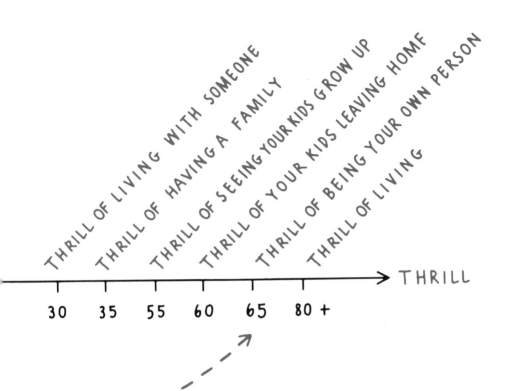

THRILL OF LIVING WITH SOMEONE

THRILL OF HAVING A FAMILY

THRILL OF SEEING YOUR KIDS GROW UP

THRILL OF YOUR KIDS LEAVING HOME

THRILL OF BEING YOUR OWN PERSON

THRILL OF LIVING

→ THRILL

30   35   55   60   65   80 +

MASTER
OF YOUR
LIFE!

What can you learn from twenty-year-olds about roommates, downsizing, living frugally, making new friends, learning new skills, and traveling? What can you learn from sixty-five-year-olds about roommates, downsizing, living frugally, making new friends, learning new skills, and traveling?

What a perfect opportunity to design your life and to learn from each other.

SAME AND DIFFERENT

Today's new older age is very different from that of our parents and grandparents, but it's not that different from the experience of our kids.

John Zapolski coined this notion beautifully during our codesign work—Same, Different. The older adults we were codesigning with were telling us, "If you want to understand what we want, think no further than what you want. Love, purpose, well-being, and friendship. We are the same. What's different is what we need to get them."

This idea—Same, Different—became the unifying principle that would form the backbone of our TSF research and, eventually, of this book. At its core, it says that we all want the same things regardless of our age—love, purpose, well-being, and friendship. These desires are ageless.

love LOVE

purpose PURPOSE

well-being WELL-BEING

friendship FRIENDSHIP

IN THE FOLLOWING PAGES,
YOU WILL FIND WHAT
WE HAVE LEARNED ABOUT
LOVE, PURPOSE, WELL-
BEING, AND FRIENDSHIP
FROM PEOPLE WHO HAVE
LIVED, WORKED, AND
LOVED THE LONGEST.

VE

TRANSFORMATION OF LOVE

Codesigning with older people has changed the way I think about love after sixty-five. These people were honest, confident, funny, vulnerable, strong, and not shy when designing their love lives. They looked for love, sometimes in the most endearing places, like the men's department at Macy's. They wanted to share a life, but not necessarily a house. They were seduced by the idea of seduction, while remaining perfectly happy on their own.

During our long lives, love transforms from selfless love to self-love. Early in our lives, we give our all to our partners and, if we have them, to our children, often without holding much back. Our identities expand to include being a partner, wife, husband, mom, or dad.

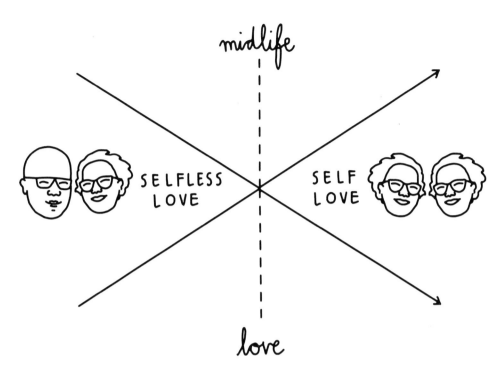

midlife

SELFLESS LOVE

SELF LOVE

love

LOVE IS NOT ONLY LOVING OTHERS—IT'S ALSO LOVING YOURSELF. IT'S COEXISTING WITH SOMEONE WITHOUT LOSING YOUR IDENTITY—DOING GOOD FOR OTHERS BUT ALSO FOR YOURSELF, EXPRESSING YOUR LOVE TOWARD OTHER PEOPLE AS WELL AS YOURSELF.

As we grow older, we accept ourselves more. We learn to have more self-compassion. We still try to do our best, but we are also okay if we don't—we forgive ourselves more easily and move on. All those years of living with ourselves helps us have the courage to be our authentic selves. We embrace our superpowers as well as our kryptonite (more on that on page 151).

Cindy Gallop is a great example of self-love. Learn more about her self-love story on page 52.

LOVE IS AN EXPERIENCE

20s	30s	60s
YOUNG LOVE	MIDLIFE LOVE	LATE LOVE

When you're in a room full of people who've spent a lifetime loving and who are still interested in designing their love lives, whether with their partner of many years or with someone new, you need a new word to describe what you're hearing. So I made up a word—Lovexperience.

Lovexperience is the combination of love and experience, of course. When you've spent thirty or forty-plus years in relationships, you have experience. You're an expert.

And with that level of expertise, you suffer fools less. You're less interested in merging homes, let alone merging your personality with another human being. You're more protective of your own "space." And generally—especially for women—you're not interested in becoming the de facto caregiver.

There is also another side to Lovexperience, which is about creating experiences together. You attract each other with your savviness, your history, your stories, your wisdom, your humor, your wit, your kindness. Your inner beauty—the beauty that comes from knowing and accepting yourself—becomes as important as your outer beauty.

You distill all that lovexperience to create new experiences of love together. You're the expert and the beginner.

These are lessons we can all benefit from—
1. Loving ourselves
2. Loving the other without losing our sense of identity
3. Being seduced by inner beauty

A LIFE OF LOVE

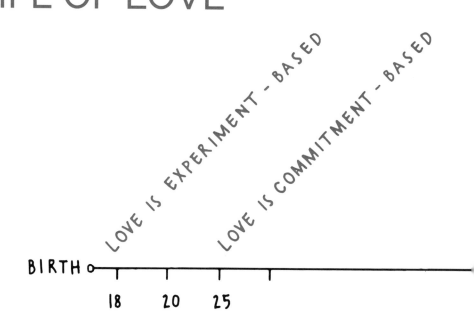

BIRTH

LOVE IS EXPERIMENT-BASED

LOVE IS COMMITMENT-BASED

18   20   25

Whether they are maintaining a relationship with the same person from early or midlife, or looking for new love, older people want to view love differently and experience it anew.

Younger people often forget about or are uncomfortable with the idea of older people wanting and having intimacy. This partly explains why dating apps, developed with a younger audience in mind, are not designed for older people. But wouldn't it be great if they were designed for everyone?

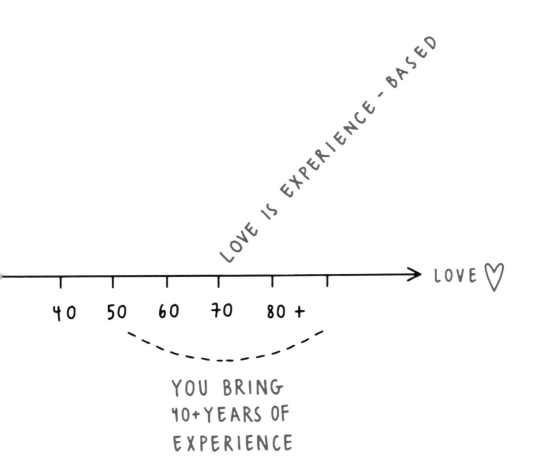

LOVE IS EXPERIENCE - BASED

40   50   60   70   80 +   LOVE ♡

YOU BRING
40+YEARS OF
EXPERIENCE

"For old people beauty doesn't come free with the hormones, the way it does for the young. . . . It has to do with who the person is."—Ursula K. Le Guin

CINDY
GALLOP

"People find it generally astonishing that I've no desire to be in love. I mean, that's how much love has been represented as the be-all-end-all of us."
—Cindy Gallop

CINDY GALLOP

Cindy Gallop is sixty-two and calls herself a proudly visible member of the most invisible segment of society—older women.

She doesn't give a damn what anyone else thinks and says that, at this age, it's a joy to do whatever the hell you want.

A British-born New Yorker, she's one of the most original people I have ever met. Cindy lives to the beat of her own drum. After a long career as one of the most powerful and successful ad executives on Madison Avenue, the mecca of advertising, she started her own company, MakeLoveNotPorn—the world's first user-generated, human-curated social sex platform.

When I talked to her about love, she smiled and said she finds it very entertaining that I would seek her advice on love since she has zero desire for what most of us call "romantic love." She has come to the realization, after all her years of living, that she's happiest on her own. She has plenty of other forms of love, including family and friends, and a current business that is all about celebrating love, but she knows she is unusual in her lack of interest in being in love.

Cindy wants people to question their beliefs and to think independently, beyond what they're socially conditioned to do. In her view, why conform to anyone's expectations when you can live life differently and still be very happy? "I project publicly everything about how I've chosen to live, because people, especially younger people, need to see this as early as possible. Older people realize they can live life on their own terms, and that's bloody wonderful. We get more desirable as we get older because we don't give a shit. I encourage both women and men, but especially women, as ageism affects us more."

Cindy, who dates younger men, says her principles for how she conducts her casual dating life would be of enormous benefit to people of all ages, whether they're looking for their soul mate or just to have some good, healthy fun.

CINDY GALLOP'S PATENTED GUIDE TO DATING, AT ANY AGE

First, they must be a nice person. Cindy says that people looking to date usually have a checklist full of things like "must have a job" or "must be driven and ambitious," but very rarely does it include "must be a very nice person." No matter how casual the relationship or what age the participants, her most fundamental criterion is that they must be a very nice person. Everybody who wants to find a great relationship would benefit from making that the number one checkbox on their dating list.

Second, she notes that most people are looking for socially endorsed attractiveness. They think about what their friends would think if they walked into a party with this person on their arm. Cindy recommends that you strip out what society has conditioned you to think about whom you should be seen with and really, genuinely look at how you respond—without any of that additional social consciousness.

Third, you should reframe how you evaluate your dates. One of the ways in which people evaluate first dates, especially if they are female, is whether both participants got "equal airtime"—did the other person ask about me as much as I asked about them? Instead, when Cindy meets younger men on that first date, the last thing she wants to do is talk about herself. She says, "I just want to hear all about him. No one is as interested in them as I am, and because of that, I hear amazing stories. One of the things I love about online dating is it enables you to meet people you would never normally meet in your everyday walk of life."

Now for Cindy's step-by-step process on how to progress from meeting someone online to meeting them, as she says it, IRL (In Real Life), turn the page.

CINDY GALLOP'S DATING FILTERS

CINDY GALLOP'S
PATENTED 3-STEP GUIDE
TO SUCCESSFUL ONLINE DATING

1. PHOTO → 2. EMAIL → 3. PHONE

IRL
(IN REAL LIFE)

CINDY GALLOP IS ON TO
SOMETHING. ACCORDING TO
JON BIRGER, AUTHOR OF
MAKE YOUR MOVE, WOMEN
SHOULD THINK ABOUT
DATING YOUNGER MEN. IN
FACT, THE TRADITIONAL
OLDER MEN—YOUNGER
WOMEN NORM IS REVERSED
WHEN OLDER WOMEN
MAKE THE FIRST MOVE. HIS
THEORY IS BACKED BY DALE
MARKOWITZ, A DATA
ANALYST ON OKCUPID,
WHO NOTES THAT WHEN
OLDER WOMEN MESSAGE
YOUNGER MEN, "THEY'RE
KILLING IT."

Here is Cindy's three-step guide to online dating:

Filter #1 is photographic. Ask for three up-to-date photos, including one full-body image. In case of refusal, take them off your list.

Filter #2 is written communication, preferably email, to establish chemistry in writing. If their writing style doesn't work for you, take them off your list.

Filter #3 is talking on the phone. You can tell a lot about someone from having a conversation with them on the phone. If you can't, hang up and take them off your list. If you have phone chemistry, proceed to meet them IRL (In Real Life).

LOVE IN AN EMPTY NEST

Not all people are looking for a new love in older age—some are seeking to rekindle one they already have. Steve and Pam D'Amico met when they were nineteen and seventeen, respectively. They've been together ever since. Steve came to my Design the Life You Love Workshop, and when he went home, taught Pam the process. They've been designing their lives together every Sunday since.

One of the reasons Steve was so eager to try the process of actively designing life was because he knew they were coming up on a life-changing event—their youngest daughter was going to college. Steve and Pam were just on the cusp of a transition and feeling rather disconnected as a couple.

Designing their lives as a couple forced them to pause and really talk to each other about where they were individually and as empty nesters.

For Pam, this was a good way of falling *back* in love with each other. By designing life together, they were each reminded of what attracted them to the other person and what brought them together. In essence, they were just good reminders of, "Yeah, we need to kind of work on that right now."

For Steve, these transition points—when you have to rediscover each other—are the natural moments when designing your life makes a lot of sense.

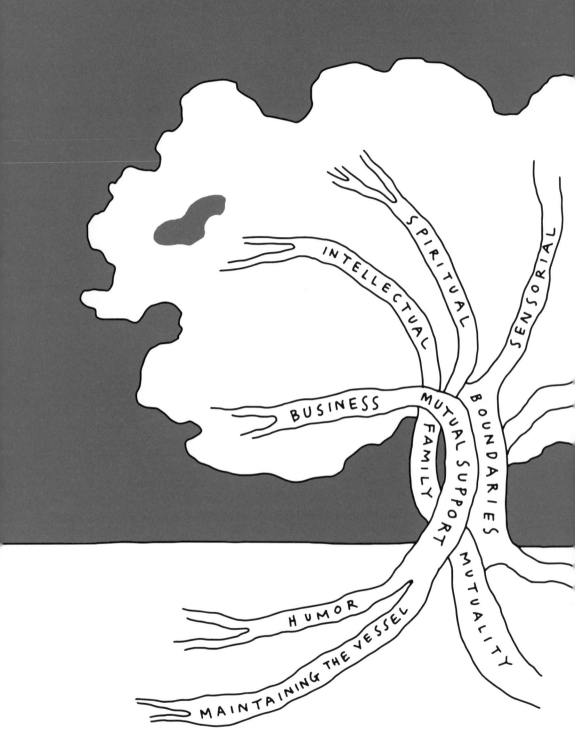

PAM AND STEVE USE A
METAPHOR OF A TREE—
TWO VINES WITH STRONG
ROOTS (HEALTH)
WRAPPED TOGETHER TO
FORM A SINGLE TRUNK
(CONNECTION) THAT
BRANCHES OUT INTO THE
FUTURE (EXPLORATION).
THIS WAY OF SEEING THE
WORLD SERVED AS A
REMINDER THAT THEY
COULD DO THIS AS A
COUPLE, BUT WITH THE
NEED FOR BOTH MUTUALITY
AND DIFFERENTIATION.

TRAVEL

REST AND RELAXATION

MIND-BODY CONNECTION

EXPLORATION
CONNECTION
HEALTH

PURP

POSE

TRANSFORMATION OF PURPOSE

While codesigning life with older people, we observed their deep sense of purpose that came from within—from helping others, starting something new, and doing what they love. Even in the absence of external drivers, like work or children, they find meaning.

When we're younger, we derive our sense of purpose from well-defined organizations, like school, office, home, or places of worship. I call these *ready-made purpose.* These structures lose their importance, recede, or disappear in later life as we retire or have second careers, become empty nesters, or downsize. Our sense of purpose starts to come from within, which I call *self-made purpose.*

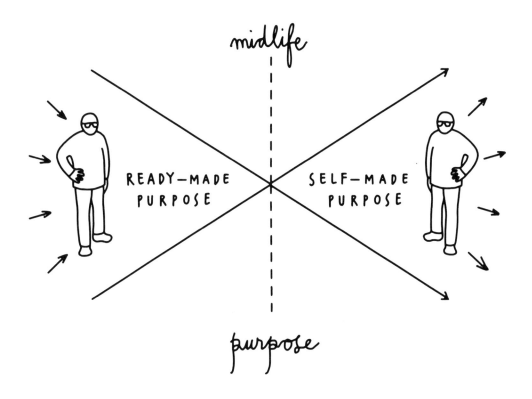

midlife

READY—MADE PURPOSE   SELF—MADE PURPOSE

purpose

Older people we codesigned with told us they start new projects and finish old ones. They said they now have time to help others, so they volunteer, help younger family members, or fight for a cause they believe in. They enjoy teaching as much as learning and hone their creativity and imagination. For many, doing what they love becomes a guiding principle.

WHAT ARE YOUR READY-MADE PURPOSE? YOUR SELF-MADE PURPOSE?

Ready- or self-made, our purpose is a continuum. Deriving meaning from what we do has no age.

A LIFE OF PURPOSE

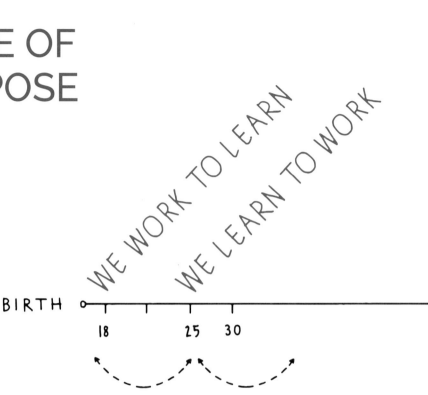

Draw a line (like the one above) that begins at birth and ends at finding your purpose, and map your life of purpose.

When I did it, I noticed an interesting pattern.

When we're students and our life is mostly about going to school . . . *we work to learn.*

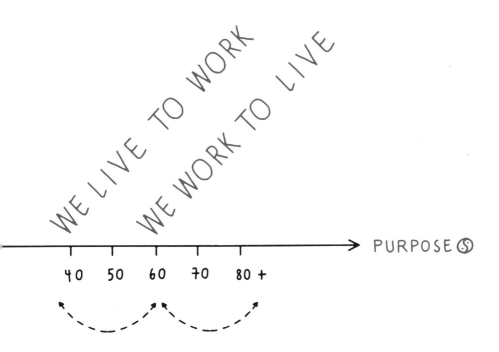

WE LIVE TO WORK

WE WORK TO LIVE

PURPOSE ⑤

40   50   60   70   80 +

When we leave school, look for a job, and start working . . . *we learn to work.*

As we take on new responsibilities, like having a family or taking care of our elders, our work and life become one . . . *we live to work.*

As we grow older and become wiser, doing what we love, helping others, and being kind to ourselves, purpose becomes more important and . . . *we work to live our best lives.*

WORK REIMAGINED

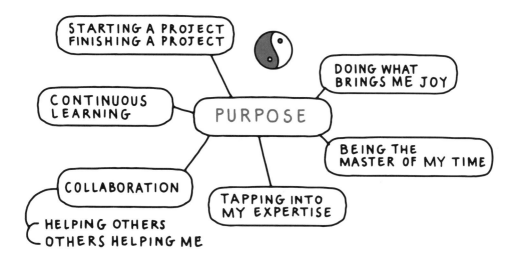

STARTING A PROJECT
FINISHING A PROJECT

DOING WHAT
BRINGS ME JOY

CONTINUOUS
LEARNING

PURPOSE

BEING THE
MASTER OF MY TIME

COLLABORATION

TAPPING INTO
MY EXPERTISE

HELPING OTHERS
OTHERS HELPING ME

Throughout life we evolve from students to novices to experts to masters of our work, all of which leads to wisdom.

Part of the wisdom that comes from experience is realizing you don't have to wait to be older to do what you love. You can be intentional about being the master of your time. You can lean into your expertise. You can help others—helping others helps us. You can practice reciprocity—teach and learn, help and be helped, give and take.

CREATING MEANING

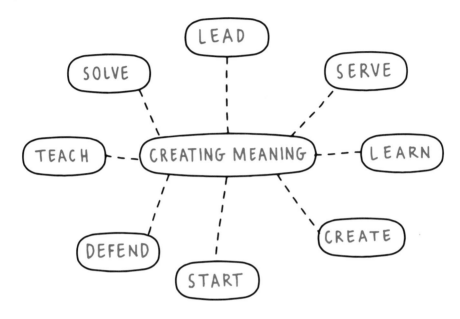

Having purpose is about creating meaning.
Creating meaning is motivating and energizing.
It gets us out of bed every morning.

Here are eight ways you can create meaning.
Which are you currently practicing?
Which will you add as you design your
longer life? Which did I miss?

DOING WHAT MAKES YOU COME ALIVE

01. create time for what you love

02. waste less time

03. share your knowledge

04. care less what people think

The work that brings us joy sits between creating more time to do what we love and having less time to waste—having more experience, expertise, and wisdom while caring less about what others think.

I repeat. Create more time to do what you love. Waste less time. Share more of your expertise. Care less about what others think.

There are many lessons I learned from teaching older adults how to design their lives. That's why I wrote this book. But this one is magical—the one I want my kids to practice.

LIFE PHASES
THAT REPEAT

REPEAT

BIRTH

FAMILY

STABILITY
HAVING KIDS
WORKING
UPSIZING
SECURITY

EARLY ADULTHOOD

FREEDOM
SEX
LEARNING
DOWNSIZING
NEW EXPERIENCES

My friend and colleague Leah Caplan wisely
says, "The day our kids fly the coop is when
we will get back our life."

Kids fly the coop. We can too!

REPEAT

LIFE

FAMILY

STABILITY
HAVING KIDS
WORKING
UPSIZING
SECURITY

LATE ADULTHOOD

FREEDOM
SEX
LEARNING
DOWNSIZING
NEW EXPERIENCES

For many of us, with or without children, late adulthood is the second time in our lives when we have a new period opening up in front of us—one we can fill with education and learning; travel and exploration; new places, cities, and countries; and new friendships and relationships.

MARSHALL GOLDSMITH

"I've learned it's never too late to reflect, because as long as you're breathing you have more time. But it's never too early as well— and early is better."

—Marshall Goldsmith,

The Earned Life

MARSHALL GOLDSMITH

Marshall Goldsmith is known as the world's number one leadership coach. He calls himself a new age monk but looks and acts like Santa, with an unparalleled generosity for giving the gift of knowledge and teaching everyone what he knows.

Marshall has designed and redesigned the life he loves. (Full disclosure, I am Marshall's life coach, and he came up with the inspiration for his 100 Coaches in my workshop.)

Marshall's book *The Earned Life* is based, like all his books, on the Buddhist philosophy of impermanence. Marshall says that every time you take a breath, it's a new you.

There is no such thing as the permanent you. We all are always changing. Life is constantly a restart; every breath is a restart.

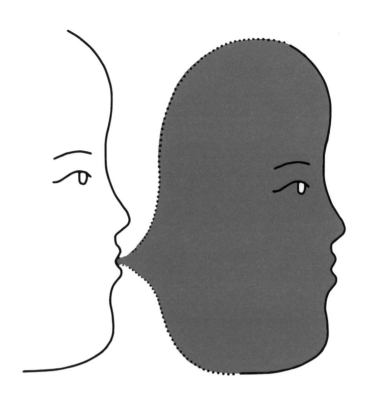

EVERY BREATH IS A NEW you.

Marshall works with some of the most successful people in the world. In his experience, when these CEOs retire or great athletes win the gold, depression, anxiety, and frustration ensue. The reason is because these figures are all focused on a goal that has a timeline. But once you achieve the goal or cross the finish line, you think, *Now what?*

There is a way to avoid that sense of confusion or disappointment. Instead of focusing just on big moments, like retirement, as a restart, you can realize that life is constantly a restart, every breath is a restart. We're always restarting.

As Marshall teaches us, if you want to lead a great life, make peace with the fact there's no winning if you think of it as a game of "I will be happy when . . ." Realize that it's all about now, whether you're eighteen or eighty-five. Nirvana is right here and right now.

When I asked Marshall about how we can make this thinking into a habit, he said the key is to frame things in what he calls *active questions.* Don't ask yourself, "Am I happy?" Ask instead, "Did I try my best to be happy?" The key is trying your best and knowing that every breath, every day, is a restart.

DID I TRY
MY BEST
TO BE
happy?

Marshall gives the example of Safi Bahcall, the physicist, entrepreneur, and best-selling author. Safi made a great breakthrough when he realized that achievement is an independent variable related to happiness. He always thought happiness was a function of achievement. *So*, he thought, *if I achieve more, I will be happy. And to be happy I need to achieve more.* His life was a constant treadmill—he's sold millions of books, he's got more degrees than you can count, and he has the IQ of one in a million. So, when is he going to hit the finish line? He's not! By tying happiness to achievement, he's a hamster, just spinning around on a wheel. Then he finally realized that achievement is good and happiness is good. But they're not the same.

HOW TO RESTART EVERY DAY

The beauty of Marshall's philosophy of an earned life is that it is ageless. Regardless of our physical age, we are always restarting. And the sooner we learn this, the better.

Marshall developed his daily questions as a tool to practice a beginner's mind every day. The inspiration came from Kelly Goldsmith, his daughter, a onetime contestant on the reality competition show *Survivor* and now a tenured professor of marketing. Kelly pointed out to Marshall that almost all employee engagement questions are passive questions like, "Do you have clear goals?" When you ask a passive question and the answer is negative, you tend to find fault in others—like, "I don't have clear goals because my boss didn't give them to me." When you ask an active question—"Did I do my best to have clear goals?"—there's no "them." You're not judging anybody else; you're just talking about you.

Active questions help us take responsibility for our own lives and sense of meaning, which of course is the foundation of designing an original life.

MARSHALL GOLDSMITH'S 6 DAILY QUESTIONS

Did I try my best to...

- SET CLEAR GOALS
- MAKE PROGRESS TOWARD GOAL ACHIEVEMENT
- BE HAPPY
- FIND MEANING
- BUILD POSITIVE RELATIONSHIPS
- BE FULLY ENGAGED

I PRACTICE MARSHALL'S DAILY QUESTIONS EVERY DAY WITH MY FRIEND SCOTT OSMAN, CEO OF 100 COACHES. IT IS A SIMPLE EXERCISE, AND YOU CAN PRACTICE IT TOO. SET FIVE TO TEN MINUTES ON YOUR CALENDAR WITH A FRIEND. ADD YOUR OWN QUESTIONS TO MARSHALL'S SIX QUESTIONS. MINE ARE THINGS LIKE, "DID I DO MY BEST TO CALL MY MOM EVERY DAY?" AND "DID I DO MY BEST TO DRAW SOMETHING AND SHARE?"

I ASK SCOTT HIS QUESTIONS, AND HE GIVES HIMSELF A RATING ON A SCALE OF 1–10. AND THEN WE SWITCH. IT'S A DAILY REMINDER THAT EVERY DAY IS A RESTART.

DOING WHAT YOU LOVE

Stuart Crainer, cofounder of Thinkers50, once told me that the work he loves doing is creating something from nothing. In reality, though, very little of his time is devoted to what he loves—the beginning (when you have the idea) and the end (when you have the result).

Cognitive psychology tells us that doing something you love, small or big, is a cornerstone of happiness. We all deserve to work on something we love. Older people we designed with were often a little wistful when it came to talking about their work and purpose. Most of them expressed the sentiment that they wanted to work on something they love, since they didn't always get to do so when they were younger.

Why do we tell ourselves we will do the work we love later in life? It would be better if we gave ourselves permission to do something that matters to us at any age.

CREATING
SOMETHING
FROM
NOTHING

To get started on something you love,
turn the page.

MICHAEL BUNGAY
STANIER

"This is your one and precious life. I want you to do something with it. Not because you're a bad person if you don't, but if you do, you might find a more interesting version of yourself, a more complete, expanded, thrilling version of yourself. And you might also make the world a bit better for yourself, for others, and for me. If I've got a lot of people doing worthy goals, the world's going to be a bit better as a result of that."

—Michael Bungay Stanier

STARTING
SOMETHING NEW

I reached out to Michael Bungay Stanier about how to start something that matters. Michael is the best-selling author of *The Coaching Habit* and a master at starting and finishing projects. Another of his books, *How to Begin*, says right on the cover: OPEN THE BOOK AND START DOING SOMETHING THAT MATTERS.

Michael says people often don't start something because they can't see how it will finish. If they don't know how it finishes, they don't want to start, because what if they start and it goes nowhere? What if it fails? What if the ending isn't what they want the ending to be? That sense of ambiguity and uncertainty can stop us from beginning.

He says that many times, when we start things, we hope it's a little bit like Google Maps. You'd like to type a destination in and receive the exact route, the exact number of minutes, where the coffee shop is, and an alternative route if you need it.

Since that app doesn't exist (yet), one way to start something new is to give yourself permission to say, "I don't know how this will end."

WORK ON WHAT GIVES YOU JOY

Michael's trick to get over the ambiguity of not knowing how something will end is to work in six-week bursts. He makes a commitment of six weeks and asks himself what it would be like to work on this project or idea for six weeks. At the end of six weeks, he stops and asks, "How's it going? Where am I now, and is this still the right thing to do? And what would I do over the next six weeks to move this forward in a helpful way?"

Six weeks is just the right amount of time—long enough to actually make some real progress on something and short enough that you don't feel the opportunity cost is too great. Michael says if it turns out you've been working on the wrong stuff for six weeks, the worst that happens is you just wasted six weeks. And, of course, nothing's ever really wasted. Everything comes back one way or another.

It is never too early or too late to do something you love. Give yourself permission to work on things that give you joy. You might transform people's lives in the process, including your own.

I CAN START A NEW PROJECT!

EVEN IF I DON'T KNOW HOW IT WILL END!

GREAT *ambiguity* PROJECTS

Michael Bungay Stanier's Tips on how to start something new:

1. Start even if you don't know how it will end. Often great projects are the ones we know how to start but don't know the ending to.

2. Ambiguity is okay. Don't expect Google Maps to tell you what to expect on this journey.

3. Work in small bursts of time or cycles and then stop and check if the work is still meaningful. Adjust and continue.

WELL-

BEING

WELL-BEING

When my kids were little, and I was working and mothering like crazy in New York City, a friend of mine who had older daughters took me out to lunch. I was exhausted, and for someone who teaches people how to design their lives, I wasn't doing such a great job with mine. I asked my friend if she had any advice for me. She looked into my eyes and said, "Call out the good moments."

Today, if you ask my kids my favorite expression, they'll say in unison, "This is a good moment!"

The older adults who codesigned their lives with my team also talked to us about their good moments. One woman told us her good moments are sitting in an old swivel chair in a hunting cabin her brother-in-law built for her in the middle of the forest, quietly waiting for her prey. Another told us about UFOs, Unfinished Objects, and how they gather two to three times a year to finish unfinished objects, like quilts, with her community. Another woman talked about the pleasure of dancing with a group of younger people in Central Park.

THIS CHAPTER IS ABOUT CULTIVATING THE KIND OF WELL-BEING THAT COMES FROM RECOGNIZING THE GOOD MOMENTS.

I LIKE AN EASYGOING MEAL WITH
BELOVED FAMILY MEMBERS + FRIENDS
ON A BALMY SUMMER DAY AROUND
GOOD FOOD SOMEONE ELSE HAS MADE
WHERE WE INVARIABLY EAT AND TALK
AS THE SUN GOES DOWN, AND THE MOON
COMES UP, PLATES AND GLASSES ARE
EMPTIED AND REFILLED. IT GOES ON
FOR A LONG TIME, STORIES ARE TOLD,
PEOPLE REMEMBERED, FOOD IS PASSED
AROUND, AND THERE SEEMS TO BE NO END
TO IT. OUR ELDERS AND OUR KIDS, OUR AND
THEIR FRIENDS, SMILING, LAUGHING,
FEELING LIKE THIS IS THE ONLY PLACE ON EARTH.

this is a good moment

TRANSFORMATION OF WELL-BEING

When we are younger, our well-being is about body over mind. As we grow older, our well-being is about mind over body.

It is as if our minds compensate for our older bodies, honing them to be wiser. We are less driven by external motivators and are more motivated from within, driven to be our best selves. We practice self-acceptance, gratitude, generosity, being in the present, and appreciating the small stuff. In other words, we get more skilled at creating our conditions for joy.

What we learned from older people who designed their lives can inspire us to practice this kind of well-being at any age. Why wait?

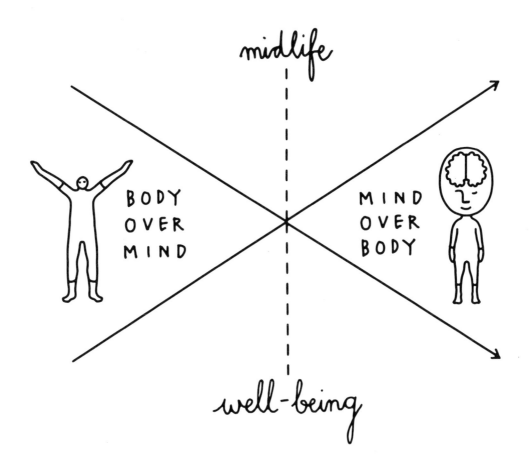

midlife

BODY
OVER
MIND

MIND
OVER
BODY

well-being

WELL-BEING IS NOT ONLY EXTERNAL BUT ALSO INTERNAL. IT'S REALIZING THAT HELPING OTHERS IS THE BEST WAY TO HELP YOURSELF. IT'S EXERCISING A LITTLE EVERY DAY.

IT'S ADAPTING AND ROLLING WITH THE PUNCHES AND PERSEVERING. IT'S ACCEPTING WHO YOU ARE. IT'S BEING AN OPTIMIST AND DECLARING VICTORY OVER EACH DAY.

WELL-BEING INDEX

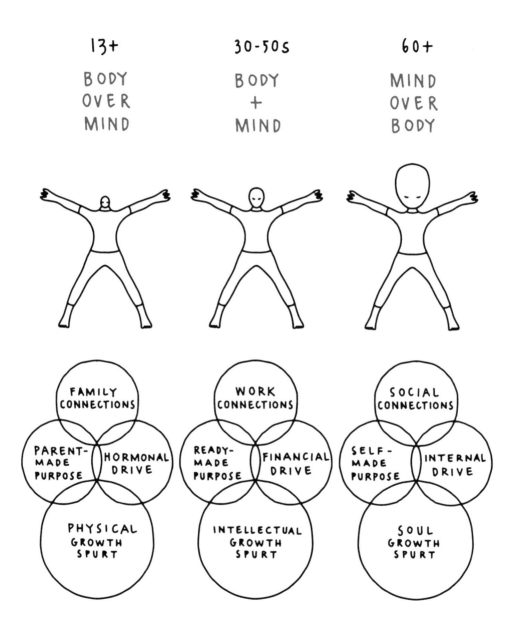

13+	30-50s	60+
BODY OVER MIND	BODY + MIND	MIND OVER BODY

FAMILY CONNECTIONS

PARENT-MADE PURPOSE · HORMONAL DRIVE

PHYSICAL GROWTH SPURT

WORK CONNECTIONS

READY-MADE PURPOSE · FINANCIAL DRIVE

INTELLECTUAL GROWTH SPURT

SOCIAL CONNECTIONS

SELF-MADE PURPOSE · INTERNAL DRIVE

SOUL GROWTH SPURT

The ingredients that make up our well-being change over time. When we're young, our life is defined by our parents, teachers, and friends.

They circumscribe our lives and our sense of purpose. On top of that, when we are young, we're in a physical growth spurt, at the mercy of our bodies and hormones. This is truly when we experience body over mind.

When we grow into adulthood, we have an intellectual growth spurt. We shape our lives, finding work and creating family. In return, our lives are defined by the rhythms of work and family, both of which fuel our sense of purpose. We seem to reach an equilibrium between our bodies and minds.

When we're older, we have a soul growth spurt. Our purpose is often self-made and more about being of service to others, whether we're retiring or starting a second or third career. Our lives are largely motivated intrinsically rather than extrinsically.

We practice mind over body.

CRYSTALLIZED
INTELLIGENCE

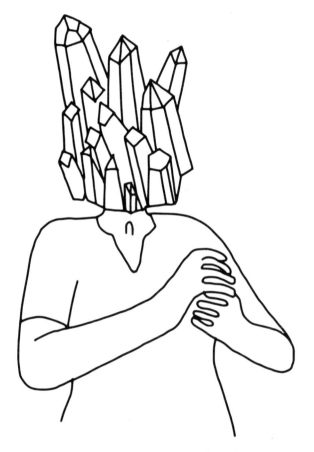

crystallized intelligence

The first time I read about crystallized intelligence was in an article about design and aging in *Fast Company*, written by Don Norman, the author of *The Design of Everyday Things*. He writes, "As we age, we have more experience with life, which can make us better decision-makers and managers. Crystallized intelligence, it is called, and it gets better with experience. A caveat is that we often face physical changes that designers fail to account for into their work."

Cognitive psychology explains the wisdom we associate with older people in terms of crystallized intelligence—the sum of learned processes and knowledge that is a direct outcome of experience. We get better at making decisions as we get older because of our experience. The longer we live, the more experience we have, and the better we become at decision-making. No wonder that my eighty-plus-year-old uncle, Gün Birsel, is my go-to person whenever life throws me a curveball!

Use your crystallized intelligence, or reach out to someone older, when you too need help with better decision-making.

"Research demonstrates that older adults have more crystallized intelligence as reflected in semantic knowledge, vocabulary, and language. As a result, adults generally outperform younger people on measures of history, geography, and even on crossword puzzles, where this information is useful (Salthouse, 2004). It is this superior knowledge, combined with a slower and more complete processing style, along with a more sophisticated understanding of the workings of the world around them, that gives older adults the advantage of 'wisdom' over the advantages of fluid intelligence, which favors the young (Baltes, Staudinger, & Lindenberger, 1999; Scheibe, Kunzmann, & Baltes, 2009).*"

*MARTHA LALLY AND SUZANNE VALENTINE-FRENCH, LIFESPAN DEVELOPMENT:

A PSYCHOLOGICAL PERSPECTIVE, 2ND EDITION, 2019, UNDER CREATIVE COMMONS

ATTRIBUTION-NONCOMMERCIAL-SHARE ALIKE 3.0 UNPORTED LICENSE

(HTTP://CREATIVECOMMONS.ORG/LICENSES/BY-NC-SA/3.0/).

DECONSTRUCTION OF WELL-BEING

Well-being is both mind and body.

Think about these prompts as a checklist for your own well-being. How are you taking care of your mind? Your body? What are you grateful for—people and things? Where's your purpose coming from? What do you do to be in the present? What are the social connections that help you feel connected to others and to your purpose?

FEEL FREE TO ADD TO THIS DECONSTRUCTION.

SEX, DRUGS,
AND ROCK AND ROLL

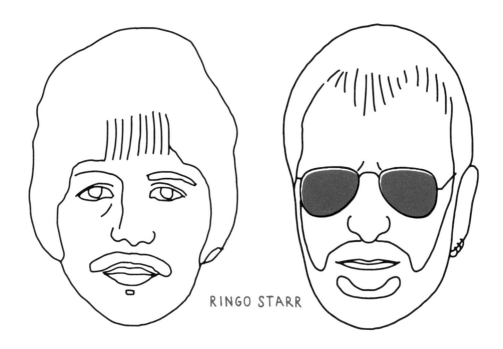

RINGO STARR

If we're Same, Different, our understanding of our well-being also needs to be reconsidered and reinvented for long life.

Think, for example, of what comes to your mind when you read *sex, drugs, and rock and roll*. Your kid, nephew, or niece who is in their twenties, or your parents, or friends in their sixties? If you said both, you wouldn't be wrong.

Young people and older people are practicing sex, drugs, and rock and roll (or dancing to it), albeit differently. If this feels counterintuitive, especially for older people, think again.

Menopause products are a $1 billion industry, according to a 2021 article in *Bloomberg*. When you turn the page, you will find an article about Z Reitano, whose company, Ro, started with ED (erectile dysfunction) medicine (for older and younger men).

Recreational drug use among older people is up, with doctor-prescribed medical cannabis accounting for one-quarter of usage. Older adults (thirty-five-plus) are the biggest listeners of paid music streaming services. According to a 2017 study, dancing and the cognitive demands of learning new moves and steps improves wiring and functioning of older brains when compared to walking and stretching.

SPEAKING OF ROCK AND ROLL, I WATCHED THE BEAUTIFUL BEATLES DOCUMENTARY *GET BACK* TOGETHER WITH MY FRIEND GREG PARSONS WHO QUIPPED, "WWRD" (WHAT WOULD RINGO DO). RINGO SEEMS TO BE AS TIMELESS AS ONE CAN GET, SHOWING UP AND GETTING THE WORK DONE WITH NO FUSS AND WITH A LOT OF ELEGANCE. HE SEEMS TO BE FINE IN HIS SKIN, WHICH IS AS GOOD A DEFINITION FOR WELL-BEING AS ANY. THEN AND NOW. SO I PUT A BEATLES SONG ON AND ASK MYSELF, WWRD?

ZACHARIAH
REITANO

"I'm devoting my life to trying to re-create my dad with software, and give him to everyone, because his patient centricity truly came from a sense of love for the patient."

—Z Reitano

ZACHARIAH REITANO

happy

healthy

PATIENT-CENTERED CARE

I met Zachariah Reitano, known as Z, for a walk and talk. Z had me at, "I want to re-create my dad with software." He continued by explaining that all immediate members of his family—his dad, mom, sister, and Z himself—had life-threatening illnesses and survived, thanks to his father, who is a physician. And then he talked about erectile dysfunction.

Z is the young cofounder of Ro, a patient-centered health start-up. Like many founders, Z's approach to patient-centered care comes from his own experiences.

When Z was eighteen, he flatlined during a stress test, was revived by his dad, and immediately had a heart procedure. He survived to wake up to something equally horrendous, at least for a teenage boy. The heart medication he was prescribed had a side effect—erectile dysfunction (ED).

Luckily for Z, his dad was able to resolve what his son wanted, to have sex, with what he needed, a healthy heart, with an ED drug. This is what inspired Z to re-create his dad with software.

DESIGN OF CARE

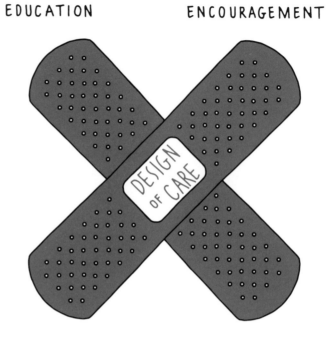

EDUCATION   ENCOURAGEMENT

DESIGN OF CARE

ENFORCEMENT   ENGINEERING

How do you design patient-centered care? And what can we learn from patient-centered care that can inform how we design our long lives?

Z and his team use a health framework for exploring how to give people what they want and what they need.

It's called the four Es.

• Education. Like a sex education campaign that teaches condom use, which then dramatically reduces the spread of sexually transmitted diseases.

• Encouragement. Like an insurance program that urges people to walk a certain number of steps in return for a deduction in their insurance policy premium.

• Enforcement. Like laws that require you to be eighteen years old to vote, twenty-one years old to drink, and twenty-five years old to rent a car.

• Engineering. Like putting vitamin B in bread, vitamin D in milk, and iodine in salt.

Where education, encouragement, and enforcement aim to *change* behavior, engineering aims to *create* a frictionless behavior. Z says their ultimate goal is to create a frictionless journey for their customers, which will lead to a healthier and longer life.

RON
CARUCCI

Designing your life means creating an authentic life, one in which you can be your true and honest self. This is the essence of well-being, especially as we age.

No one understands this better than Ron Carucci, author of *To Be Honest.*

Ron's research identified four factors— Clear Identity, Dignity in Accountability, Transparency, and Cross-Boundary Relationships—that affect honesty, justice, and purpose. When these factors are absent or ineffective, the conditions compel us to choose dishonesty and self-interest.

But when they're done well, we are sixteen times more likely to tell the truth, behave fairly, and serve a greater good.

Ron explained to me that an important part of living an honest life is reconciling the past with the future. Reconciliation is the ability to face ourselves, to acknowledge the places we haven't been honest with or about ourselves. And then, choose to be satisfied with who you are, even in the midst of regrets, and live out the future to your fullest, despite whatever is behind you.

RECONCILING PAST AND FUTURE

1. MAKE A LIST

HURT*

HURT*

HURT*

2. PICK 3

3. WRITE A LETTER

4. LET GO

5. SHARE

6. BE FREE

This step-by-step process from Ron Carucci, about reconciling your past and future, will help you develop your own sense of well-being:

1. Make an inventory. List the unresolved places where someone hurt you or where you hurt someone. These may be places in your life you've kept hidden or secret.

2. Circle the three that are the most painful. These are the ghosts that occupy your mind and haunt you the most, robbing you of joy, or of feeling proud or confident.

3. Personify them and write them a letter. Ask them for forgiveness or forgive them.

4. Let them go. Tell these ghosts their services are no longer needed in your life and that you're releasing them.

5. Share. Read your letters to someone who will listen without offering you advice. All they need to do is hold this space with you.

6. Feel free. Knowing you're not the only person holding this pain anymore is powerful. It's the beginning of the healing process and of your reconciliation.

FILL THIS SPACE WITH NEW PEOPLE, IDEAS, AND EXPERIENCES AND RESOLVE NOT TO LET THE OLD GHOSTS COME BACK.

FRIEN

DSHIP

TRANSFORMATION OF FRIENDSHIP

One of the advantages of a long life is the longevity of our friendships—friends we went to kindergarten with, played with in our old neighborhood, started university with, met when our kids started school, met through our work, or encountered in other places along the way. They're our dear old friends, and it takes years, decades, to build these friendships.

However, somewhere along the way, we often forget that we also need to make new friends or even how to make them. We become reliant on the people we know. This is a challenge, but it is also the opportunity to make "fresh" friends.

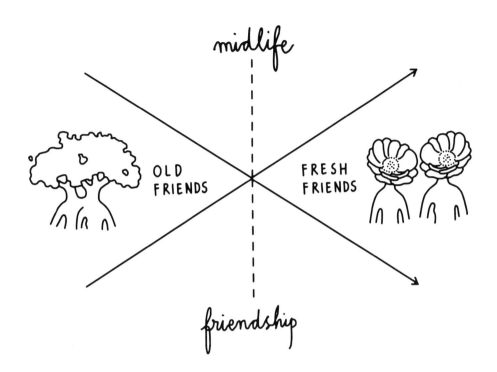

midlife

OLD
FRIENDS

FRESH
FRIENDS

friendship

Fresh friends bring with them fresh ideas, points of view, experiences, families, and broader circles of friends. Together, we get to try new things, meet new people, and experience different kinds of activities.

And if they are fresh, we are too. We are very different today from who we were ten, twenty, or thirty years ago. We know ourselves better, understand what we want, and are more comfortable in our skins.

It is never too early or too late to make fresh friends. Take it from me, an introvert at heart.

I CALL NEW FRIENDS *FRESH FRIENDS* INTENTIONALLY. IF OUR OLD FRIENDS ARE LIKE OLD TREES, AND TOGETHER WE ARE LIKE A FOREST, THESE FRESH FRIENDS ARE LIKE FLOWERS, AND TOGETHER WE MAKE A GARDEN.

A LIFE OF FRIENDSHIP

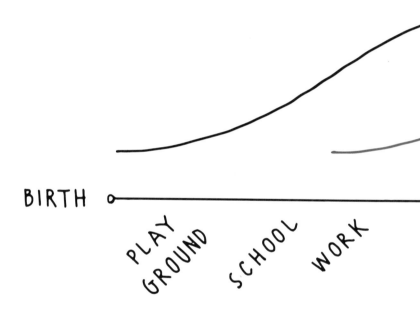

BIRTH

PLAY GROUND   SCHOOL   WORK

All our lives we make friends. Starting from our youngest age, when we make friends on playgrounds, we have social constructs that create opportunities for friendship. These recede as we grow older, but our need for friendship doesn't. How can we make new, fresh friends as we grow older?

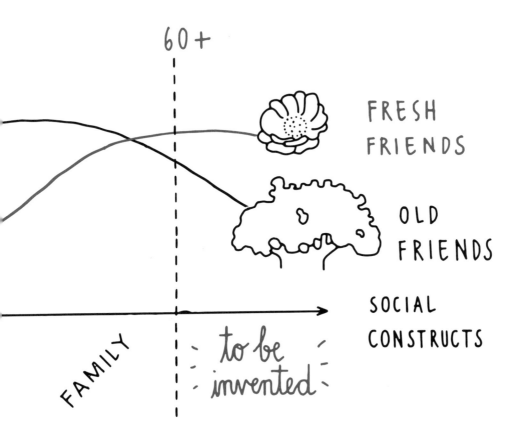

60+

FRESH
FRIENDS

OLD
FRIENDS

SOCIAL
CONSTRUCTS

FAMILY

to be
invented

MAKING FRIENDS

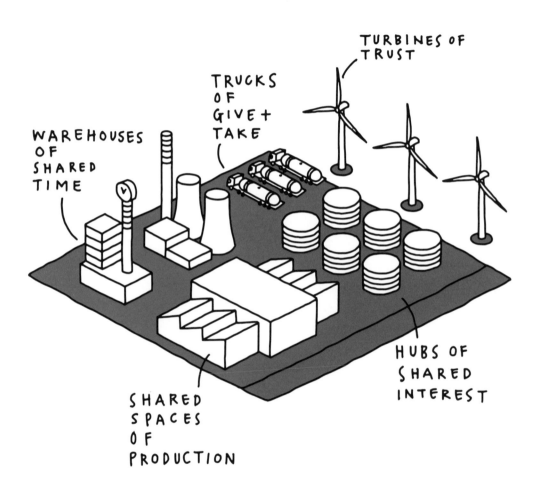

TURBINES OF
TRUST

TRUCKS
OF
GIVE +
TAKE

WAREHOUSES
OF
SHARED
TIME

SHARED
SPACES
OF
PRODUCTION

HUBS OF
SHARED
INTEREST

Unlike love, friendships are made rather than found. We all need fresh friends in addition to our old friends. Social connections are the fabric of a good life. As you're designing your life, think of a friendship factory where you can literally manufacture friends. To make friends in this factory, you need to build trust, have common interests and values, and spend time together. We all need to create fresh friends in addition to our old friends, and this metaphor is useful for thinking about how to make friends differently.

We can build trust quickly when a dependable friend introduces us to their friends. Common interests, like shared hobbies and projects—from gardening to books—bring us together. Shared values can include a cause worth fighting for or helping others through volunteering. Reciprocity accelerates friendships—when we teach or help each other without expecting anything in return. A shared space, whether a physical classroom or a digital one, where we spend time together completes the formula for friendship.

When these things come together, our chances of making new friends are much augmented.

CHIP CONLEY

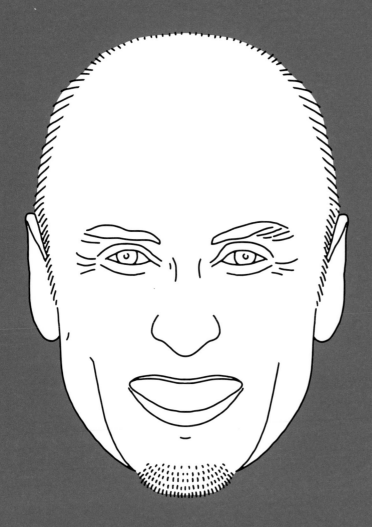

"We each evolve over the course of a life and, thus, our friendships should as well. A stagnant friendship is sort of like a stagnant pond. It smells and nothing lives there.

We want people in our lives we can grow old with, grow young with, and, ideally, just grow with."

—Chip Conley

Have you watched the movie *The Intern*?

It is the story of a young, visionary founder (Anne Hathaway) and a wise, elder intern (Robert De Niro). The reversal of roles—young boss and elder intern—and the collaboration and friendship that emerges reminds me of another intergenerational collaboration and friendship, that of Chip Conley, the hospitality maverick who at fifty-two teamed up with Brian Chesky, the young CEO of Airbnb. As Airbnb's head of global hospitality and strategy, Chip helped Brian build this start-up company into the now-iconic global hospitality brand that it is.

Chip is no intern, but he has movie star good looks and charisma, as well as the ability to practice a beginner's mind even after two decades as the CEO of his own hotel and restaurant company, Joie de Vivre. Brian says they hired Chip for his knowledge, but what they really gained was his wisdom—and friendship.

Chip notes it's time to switch up our thinking about the physics of wisdom. It's not just moving from old to young, but it's moving from young to old as well. We can learn from people both older and younger than us.

physics of wisdom

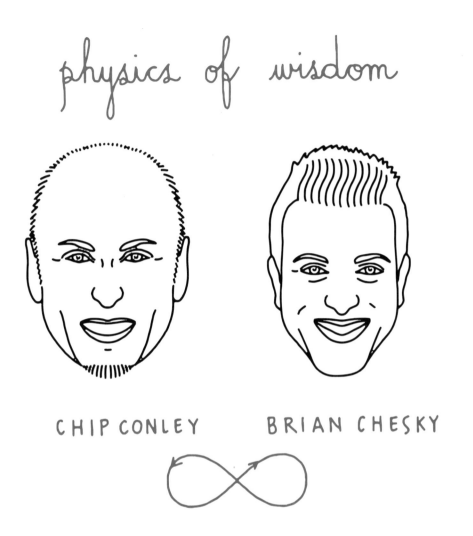

CHIP CONLEY **BRIAN CHESKY**

So in your life, who could you reach out to, to build a mutual mentorship with?

THE MODERN ELDER

Today, Chip leads Modern Elder Academy (MEA), a social entrepreneurship he founded to create a structure that allows "inspired and empowered midlifers" to get to know one another and navigate the later stages of life together.

One of the key things Chip and his team have learned in starting the academy is how starved midlifers are (average age of alums is fifty-four) for personal connection. Before MEA, the social structures to aid in making this happen just did not exist.

MEA, with two-thousand-plus alums and twenty-six regional chapters around the world, is one of the emerging models creating this social structure for midlifers and beyond.

People often arrive at the academy alone and leave having developed lifetime friendships. What turns these strangers into friends?

Chip says researchers have shown that one key element of relationships that grow close quickly, even among strangers, is what psychologist Dr. Arthur Aron calls, "sustained, escalating, personalistic, reciprocal self-disclosure." Chip adds to this idea by stating, "It's all about creating a structure that allows people to get to know each other from the inside out, instead of the outside in."

Just having a common interest—politics, modern art, professional football— makes for an interesting cocktail party conversation, but it doesn't create a close friendship. What's missing is the personal revelation and getting to know the essence of the other person.

As Chip puts it, a stranger becomes a friend when trust enters the picture, so the quicker you build trust the better. And trust in friendships is built by a combination of vulnerability and dependability.

WE OF WELLNESS

Remember how our well-being evolves from body over mind to mind over body?

Chip wants us to rethink "wellness" as being purely a personal endeavor and focus more on "social wellness," how our community and connections help support our health and well-being. This doesn't mean we shouldn't care about our diet, our workout, our sleep, and so forth, but it does mean that we should have metrics and recommendations for our depth of connections, the number of hours we're with other people per week, and how many new people we meet per month. As Chip says, "Life is a journey, but it isn't meant to be done alone."

WEllness

Illness

"Wellness starts with the letters 'WE' and Illness starts with the letter 'I.'"
—Chip Conley

PEOPLE TO GROW WITH

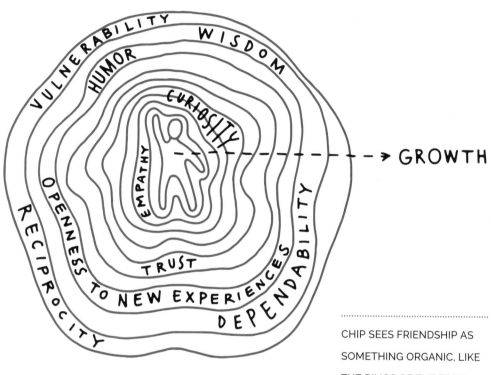

VULNERABILITY

WISDOM

HUMOR

CURIOSITY

EMPATHY

- - - → GROWTH

OPENNESS TO NEW EXPERIENCES

TRUST

RECIPROCITY

DEPENDABILITY

CHIP SEES FRIENDSHIP AS
SOMETHING ORGANIC, LIKE
THE RINGS OF THE TREE
THAT SHOW OUR AGING AND
WIZENING PROCESS AND
EVOLVE OVER THE COURSE
OF A LIFE. THE MORE RINGS,
THE STRONGER THE TREE
BECOMES, AS IT TOO BUILDS
FROM THE INSIDE OUT.

So what are the three key qualities Chip feels are needed to improve our ability to make friends later in life?

1. Curiosity, or having a strong desire to learn about others,

2. Empathy, or the ability to understand the feelings of others,

3. Openness to new experiences, or the willingness to try to embrace new ideas and things.

Note how aligned these qualities are with the principles of thinking like a designer. (see page 12).

Chip also recommends psychologist Arthur Aron's thirty-six questions, believed to accelerate intimacy between strangers to create love or deep friendship.

LEE KIM

"Whether you're an introvert or an extrovert, there has to be a threshold that you have to cross by creating something to share, whether it's a sentence, a hat, or just arranging something and taking a picture, to connect with someone."

—Lee Kim

LEE KIM

Lee Kim came to one of my weekly Design the Life You Love Virtual Teas. She was wearing a big, beautiful, sculptural hat made of pipe cleaners, and I couldn't help but notice her. Three weeks later, we met at Bryant Park. She gifted me a tall, bright red creation to go with my lipstick. As I walked home, I was approached by two women who wanted to know about my hat and took my picture, and with whom I then exchanged Instagram accounts.

The pandemic era has evened out the playing field for social life, no matter our age. Many of us have fallen out of practice in the art of making friends. We've become even more introverted (like me) from sheltering in place, or we've started working from home, or we've moved to a new place to get out of the city, be closer to nature, bring our cost of living down, or be closer to our families during these challenging times. Sometimes this means we're in a new place where we don't know many people. Frankly, we can all use some guidance about how to make fresh friends.

Lee Kim, who is a design strategist, a mom, and an extroverted introvert, has cracked the code on making fresh friends at a time when she too was feeling isolated inside a life that had become too much of a routine. Now, each time she puts a pipe cleaner hat on her head, she sends out a signal to the world: *Hi! What's your name? You wanna be my friend?*

LEE KIM'S TIPS FOR MAKING FRIENDS

1. PICK A SPACE

2. HAVE A CONVERSATION STARTER

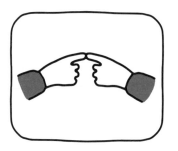

3. GO RAIN OR SHINE

4. BE READY FOR A CONVERSATION

5. KEEP IN TOUCH

6. GIVE A GIFT

Here is Lee's step-by-step guide to making fresh friends:

1. Pick your play space. When you're a kid, that space is the playground. Same here. For Lee, New York streets are her playground.

2. Bring your conversation starter, like your bright blue sand bucket or flashy jump rope at the playground. Lee's are her daily-made hats.

3. Give yourself a duration. If you're lucky, you go to the playground every day, rain or shine. Lee gave herself 365 days when she started her mission to make new friends.

4. Be prepared for a conversation. What is your, "You wanna be my friend?" conversation? Lee tells people her hat story and asks them why they thought it was interesting.

5. Keep in touch. In the playground, parents exchange phone numbers. Lee asks people for their Instagram or LinkedIn account.

6. Give a gift. At the playground you might share your candy. Lee takes off her hat and gifts it to a person every day. It's the ultimate invitation to friendship.

YOU CAN START THE PROCESS BACKWARD, BY THINKING ABOUT THE GIFT. WHAT IS SOMETHING YOU WANT TO GIFT TO STRANGERS? SOMETHING THAT COMES FROM YOUR HEART—A POEM, A PHOTO, A HAT, A FLOWER, A LESSON? FOR ME, THE VIRTUAL TEAS WHERE I TEACH PEOPLE HOW TO DESIGN THEIR LIVES HAVE BECOME MY "GIFT" FOR MAKING FRESH FRIENDS. THE PROOF IN THE PUDDING IS MY BUDDING FRIENDSHIP WITH LEE KIM.

$^-9$ YOUR AGE $^+9$

friendship formula

In one of our workshops, one of the participants taught us a memorable lesson—make friends who are nine years younger and nine years older than you are. This has since become a mantra for me and my team. It's easy to remember and speaks to the richness of having multigenerational friends in our lives.

Look around you. Who are some people who are younger and older than you with whom you can start a new friendship?

DECONSTRUCTION OF FRIENDSHIP

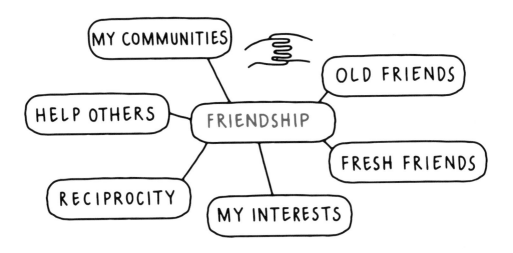

Who are your old friends, and how do you keep them close? Who are your fresh friends, and how do you make them? Are your friends multigenerational—that is to say, are some years younger and some years older than you? What are your shared interests? What's the reciprocity principle in your friendship? What do you do to help others? What are your communities?

Use these prompts to design your friendships.

PART 3.0

DESIGNING YOUR LONG LIFE

WARM-UP: WHAT BRINGS YOU JOY?

Let's start our long life project by drawing. This is a warm-up for our creativity. It's just like warming up our muscles in the gym.

If you haven't drawn something since kindergarten, that is totally okay. No masterpieces are needed here. Draw like your five-year-old self.

One of my favorite warm-ups is drawing something that brings me joy. After all, design is creating something—a product, an experience, a life—that brings us closer to joy.

Here are things that give me joy—a parade of clouds on a blue sky, a cup of hot Earl Grey tea, great art, a good book, and you, dear reader, holding this book in your hand.

What brings me joy

a parade of clouds

a cup of hot tea

Olafur Eliasson's art

a good book

and, you!

draw

write

now, your turn !

AS YOU DESIGN YOUR
LONGER LIFE, DRAW WHAT
BRINGS YOU JOY.

HOW TO BE CREATIVE EVERY DAY

To warm up your creative brain on a regular basis, you can schedule a daily creativity break into your calendar and try a different exercise each day.

1. Draw something—fruit, your coffee cup, your dog, cat, children—for five to ten minutes. Just draw. Don't judge and don't erase. My friend Ken Carbone drew an apple a day for 365 days.

2. Make a funny sculpture with objects lying on your desk. You can also collect items from your recycling bin and combine them together to make an abstract sculpture. Use a hot glue gun or lots of tape to hold it together.

3. Look up a word in the dictionary, and then look up the words that come before and after. Make up a short story using the three words (this exercise is loosely inspired by Twyla Tharp, from her book *The Creative Habit*).

4. Make new things with paper clips (earrings, letters of the alphabet, a heart). See how many things you can make in five minutes.

5. Take one photograph a day as a way to look at things around you with new eyes and create a visual memory lane. My friend Scott Osman does this using the app Day One Journal: Private Diary.

6. Draw something on your desk (e.g., your stapler) in five minutes, without looking at your hand. Cover your hand and drawing with a paper towel to help you not cheat. When done, take away the towel. Tadaaa! You'll be amazed.

For more mini creative exercises, look up
my article on INC.com referenced at the
end of the book.

Here is what I've learned from these
creative warm-ups: my thinking continues
to be more flexible and multidimentional
throughout the day when I do them.

I approach everything less fearfully (see
my Kryptonite on page 15) and more
playfully. I'm more open to seeing things
in new and unexpected ways.
And that makes all the difference.

PHYSICAL
WARM-UP

CREATIVE
WARM-UP

YOU'RE THE SUPERHERO
OF YOUR LIFE

We are the superheroes of our long lives. With that in mind, let's first deconstruct our superpowers and kryptonite.

Our superpowers are things that come easily to us. Our kryptonite are things that slow us down or deplete our superpowers. My superpowers are deconstruction and reconstruction, the process we're using here. Even as I write this book, my kryptonite is fear of failure.

Your superpowers may be curiosity, dealing with chaos, patience, or kindness. Your kryptonite may be a lack of focus, impatience, self-doubt, or procrastination. Sometimes they're the same thing—empathy is a great trait, but if we become consumed by someone else's problems, it is exhausting.

DRAW YOURSELF AS THE SUPERHERO OF YOUR LONG LIFE AND MAKE A LIST OF YOUR SUPERPOWERS AND KRYPTONITE.

Be intentional about using your super-powers, and don't beat yourself up for having kryptonite. They are both part of who we are. The longer we live, the better we get at accepting our humanness.

SUPERHEROES

MICKEY MCMANUS

Superheroes were invented in the years surrounding World War II, at a time when people felt they needed rescuing.

Superman was created in 1938, Wonder Woman in 1941, and Captain America also in 1941.

I invented the superhero exercise at a time of war too, when we were fighting for our lives during the COVID-19 pandemic.

MICKEY'S PROCESS GOES SOMETHING LIKE THIS: HE'LL FIND AN EXISTING ACTION FIGURE HE FEELS RESEMBLES HIS FRIEND. HE'LL THEN INTERVIEW FRIENDS AND FAMILY OF THIS PERSON TO GET TO THEIR ORIGIN STORY, INCLUDING THEIR SUPERPOWERS AND KRYPTONITE, HE WILL THEN HACK THE FIGURE AND ITS BOX IN BRILLIANT DETAIL TO RE-CREATE THEM AS A ONE-OF-A-KIND SUPERHERO—COMPLETE WITH THEIR UNIQUE OUTFIT, ACCESSORIES, AND STORY.

What inspired me was my friend Mickey McManus, cofounder of MAYA Design and coauthor of *Trillions*. Mickey is a designer-maker mixed with some Einstein-like genius. His favorite thing is expressing his affection for friends by custom-making their superhero action figures. At the heart of the process is researching and representing the superpowers and kryptonite of this person, which is what captivated my attention.

I thought, we cannot all have a custom-made Mickey action figure (I am still waiting for mine!). What we can do is to give ourselves the gift of knowing we each are the superheroes of our lives.

INSPIRATION

Think of those moments when you see or hear something that captures your imagination and inspires you about your life, your work, or simply the dinner you're cooking.

When I design a product, everything around me becomes a potential source of inspiration. I could go out to a museum, go to a concert, go for a walk, listen to a podcast, or talk to a friend and find inspiration. I know projects inspired by Forty-Second Street, others where the idea came to me at a Japanese street market, and one where my inspiration came from Ottoman tiles.

Inspiration is seeing parts of the solution in different places. You don't know how they're going to go together elegantly yet, but they inform you about what you want or don't want. Inspiration is a cue to what you value. And what you don't value won't inspire you.

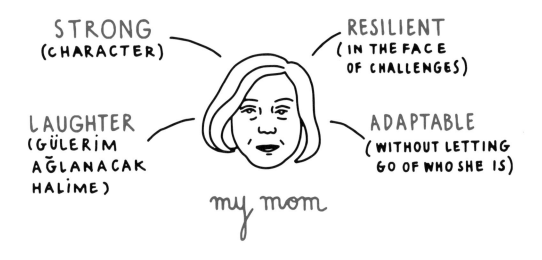

STRONG
(CHARACTER)

RESILIENT
(IN THE FACE
OF CHALLENGES)

LAUGHTER
(GÜLERİM
AĞLANACAK
HALİME)

ADAPTABLE
(WITHOUT LETTING
GO OF WHO SHE IS)

my mom

My mom, my hero.

My mother, Özgül Birsel, is resilient and strong, yet adaptable. She also defuses challenges and difficult moments with laughter.

In Turkish, we say, "I laugh through my tears," something she started doing more as she grew older. Research shows a kid laughs three hundred times a day, whereas it takes an adult two months to laugh three hundred times. We laugh much more when we are younger and older but very little between ages twenty and seventy.

My mother is my hero, and I value her ability to laugh at challenges. I now laugh more, without waiting to get to my seventies.

HEROES EXERCISE

In life, our design inspiration is other people. These are people we know, or know of. I call them *our heroes*. Our heroes tell us something about our values, beliefs, and the kinds of lives we aspire to live.

When it comes to a long life, what inspires us is older people—these *astronauts of life*—going where no one has gone before. They are our creative shortcut for what we want and what we value for our future selves.

To gather inspiration for your long life, think of your older heroes. Our heroes can be people we know, like family, friends, teachers, coaches, mentors, or mentees. They can also be people we know of, past and present, who are recognized for their contributions. They simply have something that makes us pay attention to them. They pique our interest.

FRANK LLOYD WRIGHT

FRANK LLOYD WRIGHT (FLW)
DESIGNED THE GUGGENHEIM
MUSEUM IN HIS EIGHTIES—
SOMETHING I LEARNED AS A
YOUNG DESIGN STUDENT AT
PRATT AND NEVER FORGOT.
EVER SINCE THEN, THAT'S
HOW I WANT TO BE—DO MY
BEST WORK IN MY EIGHTIES.

VALUES

MY HERO
(FLW)

MY HERO'S QUALITIES
(DOING HIS BEST WORK IN HIS 80S)

MODELING MY HERO, FLW
(DOING MY BEST WORK IN MY 80S)

The qualities we see in our heroes are our own values. That's why we notice them. They can be things like constant evolution, perseverance, having your own voice, longevity, being the best at what you love, and laughing in the face of challenges.

Values are the foundations of our ideas, whether we're designing a chair or our lives. They help us make choices and create something that matters to us.

Asking you to gather inspiration from your older heroes was my way of asking you, "What are your values around long life?" Now that you know, you can start practicing them today.

THIS EXERCISE IS A POWERFUL TOOL FOR HAVING EMPATHY FOR YOUR FUTURE SELF. WE USED IT WITH MORE THAN THREE HUNDRED DESIGNERS AND ENGINEERS AT AMAZON WHO WERE IN THEIR LATE TWENTIES AND THIRTIES TO HELP THEM HAVE EMPATHY FOR OLDER PEOPLE THEY WERE DESIGNING FOR.

DECONSTRUCTION

emotions | to avoid

challenges | opportunities

You're so good at this!

You're a natural-born deconstructionist.

You've already deconstructed your long life into your superpowers and kryptonite and values.

Let's now wrap up the deconstruction with your emotions, both positive and negative, what to avoid, and your challenges and opportunities. Remembering our challenges can also be our opportunities (for more on this, turn the page).

Deconstruction helps us see the parts that make up the whole. Once we see the parts, we can decide what we want to keep, change, or avoid.

CHALLENGES ARE OPPORTUNITIES

Challenges are opportunities.

Don't believe me? Consider the words of iconic American designer Charles Eames on the opposite page. Charles and Ray Eames used the limits of plywood to invent new furniture styles that are considered iconic and timeless today.

We all have challenges. What can set you apart from others is the willingness and enthusiasm described by Eames. If you can have the optimism to see challenges as opportunities, you will create new value. This is creativity.

Get into the habit of seeing a challenge as an opportunity. The more you practice this with everyday limitations, the better you will be at seeing things from multiple directions.

EAMES PLYWOOD LOUNGE CHAIR

"HERE IS ONE OF THE FEW
EFFECTIVE KEYS TO THE
DESIGN PROBLEM—THE
ABILITY OF THE DESIGNER
TO RECOGNIZE AS MANY
OF THE CONSTRAINTS AS
POSSIBLE—HIS WILLINGNESS
AND ENTHUSIASM FOR
WORKING WITHIN THESE
CONSTRAINTS. CONSTRAINTS
OF PRICE, OF SIZE, OF
STRENGTH, OF BALANCE, OF
SURFACE, OF TIME AND SO
FORTH."—CHARLES EAMES

That small apartment you've been complaining about is easy to clean. Your long commute is precious alone time. Asking for help is an opportunity for making friends.

Think like Pollyanna, the children's book character who sees difficulties in life cheerfully, to hone your skill in flipping challenges to opportunities.

A longer version of "Challenges are Opportunities" is in *The Freedom of Constraints: Turn Obstacles Into Opportunity* by Darcy Verhun.

EMOTIONS

What gives you joy? We started our process with a warm-up that connects our intellect to our emotions. Evryman cofounder Lucas Krump calls this taking an elevator from your brain to your heart.

Design is an intellectual process about solving complex problems. But what we want through the process is to get you to a great emotional experience—joy, ease, trust, comfort, delight . . .

Whether I am designing products for your life or helping you design the life you love, I have one word to remind me of this goal. My work is all about *love*.

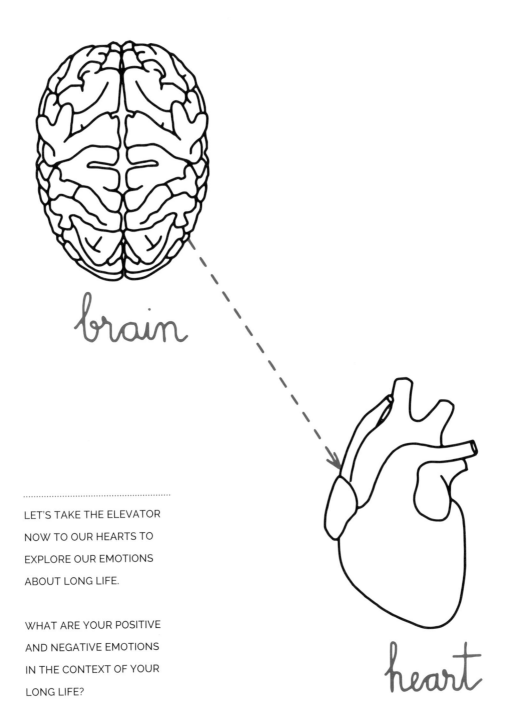

brain

heart

LET'S TAKE THE ELEVATOR
NOW TO OUR HEARTS TO
EXPLORE OUR EMOTIONS
ABOUT LONG LIFE.

WHAT ARE YOUR POSITIVE
AND NEGATIVE EMOTIONS
IN THE CONTEXT OF YOUR
LONG LIFE?

TO AVOID

2 AM

2 AM

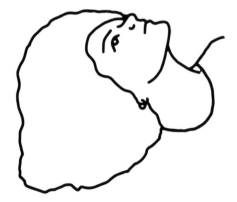

INCLUDE
8 HOURS
OF SLEEP

AVOID
LOSING
SLEEP

As you deconstruct your long life, I am sure you've come across things you wish weren't there.

We all have them—vices, conflicts, fears. We want to avoid waking up at 2:00 a.m., unable to go back to sleep, and instead want to sleep through the night. We want to banish the things that are standing in our way. We want to stop thinking negatively. People who live long are good at this.

They have no time and energy to waste on toxic friendships, suffering fools gladly, losing their identities in a relationship, ruminating endlessly, and engaging in negative self-talk, just to name a few. No wonder people who live long seem wiser. We can all learn to avoid these negative things, and the sooner the better.

WHAT DO YOU WANT TO AVOID IN THE CONTEXT OF YOUR LONG LIFE? WRITE THEM DOWN.

Decide what you want to avoid to make space, time, and resources available for more things you want to include in your life— habits, things, and people that bring you joy.

METAPHORS AS A DESIGN TOOL

In his book *VisuaLeadership*, Todd Cherches says, "A good metaphor serves to make the unfamiliar familiar, the intangible tangible, the abstract concrete, the complex simple, the confusing clear, and the invisible visible. Which is why metaphor is one of the most powerful visual thinking and visual communication methods available."

Now you know why I love metaphors as a design tool! Metaphors help us imagine an unfamiliar, intangible, abstract, complex, confusing, and invisible future and make it visible, tangible, and understandable.

work performance

IF I TELL YOU AN OFFICE IS A THEATER AND AN OFFICE SYSTEM IS ITS STAGE SET, WHAT DO YOU SEE?

WHAT I SAW BECAME THE BEGINNING OF THE RESOLVE OFFICE SYSTEM FOR HERMAN MILLER. THE THEATER METAPHOR HELPED US BREAK OUR PRECONCEPTION THAT AN OFFICE SYSTEM IS MADE UP OF CUBICLES AND INSTEAD HELPED US IMAGINE A LIGHTWEIGHT, FLEXIBLE, ADAPTABLE OFFICE SYSTEM THAT COULD CHANGE ITS CHARACTER, LOOK, AND FEEL DEPENDING ON THE PLAY BEING PERFORMED BY THE ORGANIZATION. IT CREATED A BACKDROP FOR THE PERFORMANCE OF WORK. YOU CAN THINK THIS WAY WHEN YOU'RE DESIGNING YOUR LONG LIFE TOO.

ASTRONAUTS OF LIFE

A good metaphor can help break our old preconceptions and help us see things from a new and different angle. Just like the metaphor Seda Evis coined during our research: older people are astronauts of life.

To explore this idea of being an astronaut of life, going where no one has gone before, think of space travel, real (SpaceX) or fictional (*Star Trek*, *Star Wars*).

How do you prepare for this journey? What are the superpowers that will help you be a great astronaut? What is your rocket? Your space suit? Who is your flight crew? What are their roles?

Use this metaphor to help you imagine long life in a new way at any age, but especially if you're already an astronaut of life.

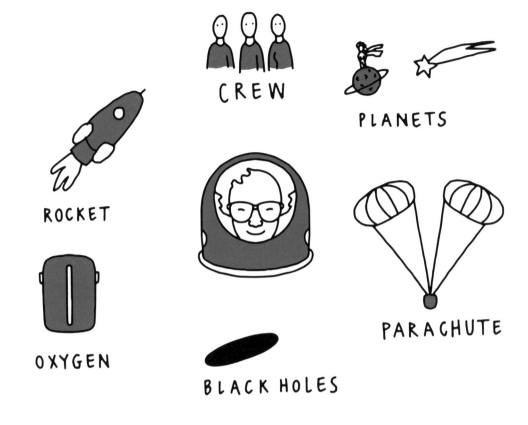

CREW

PLANETS

ROCKET

OXYGEN

BLACK HOLES

PARACHUTE

Draw yourself as the astronaut of your long life. Write down the things that the metaphor conjures up in your imagination.

You can play with this metaphor and add new, fun hooks to expand on your idea. Hooks like discovering new planets, managing limited resources, defending against hostile attacks, and time travel.

METAMORPHOSIS

Living is also being in a constant state of transition. The more we live, the more we see life as a journey, or the four seasons, or a beautiful tree.

Living through the COVID-19 pandemic, I saw life as metamorphosis. Metamorphosis is how a caterpillar (past) builds a chrysalis (present) to become a butterfly (future).

We and our lives changed through the pandemic. We were caterpillars before. Then, when we started sheltering in place, we didn't know when we could come out. As we waited, everything we knew broke down. Our lives were deconstructed.

We had plenty of time to think about what we wanted to keep, change, and get rid of. We could not go back to the way things were before.

We were transformed, perhaps more fragile but also more beautiful, with wings to help us take off and fly.

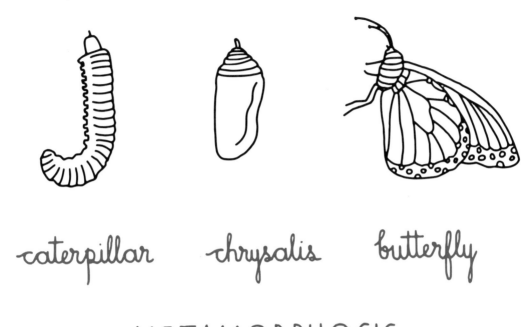

caterpillar   chrysalis   butterfly

METAMORPHOSIS

What was your metamorphosis?

What are the things you want to keep from before (caterpillar stage)?

What are the things you want to change and/or get rid of (chrysalis stage)?

What are your wings to help you take off (butterfly stage)?

LOVE EXERCISE

One of the advantages of a long life is learning to love ourselves. But what if we can learn this early on?

My friend Bill Carrier is a top executive leadership coach. He taught me this powerful self-compassion exercise, which he learned from Jack Canfield, his mentor and author of *Chicken Soup for the Soul*, that reprograms your brain to love yourself. At the end of each day, tell yourself, "I love you." Do this for a minimum of twenty-one days, until it becomes a habit.

BILL CARRIER

Bill says it takes twenty-one days for the brain to reprogram itself—if you skip one day, you need to restart. His suggestion is to combine it with another existing habit, like brushing your teeth, which will help you remember it. Bill says once you've reprogrammed your brain, you might catch yourself being self-compassionate and avoiding self-denigrating remarks like, "That was stupid of me."

You will be amazed how much better life is when you love yourself.

loving yourself

Bill Carrier's tips for teaching your brain to love yourself:

- Stand in front of the mirror right before you go to bed.
- Look yourself in the eyes and say, "I love you."
- List all the little and big things you've accomplished today.
- Say, "Good job!"
- Say, "I love you, [insert your name here]."
- Repeat for a minimum of twenty-one days.

RECONSTRUCTION

If deconstruction is about divergence, reconstruction is about convergence. It's about putting the pieces back together, knowing we cannot have everything.

To reconstruct, you need to pick your essentials, the essence of what you love, and leave out the things that are not necessary or are to be avoided.

The longer we live, the finer our crystallized intelligence becomes and the greater our self-compassion. It is easier to know our essentials. We reflect more, learn from our successes and failures, and lean more readily into things that are important to us.

Having said that, there's no reason not to start earlier and practice this simple tool for achieving simplicity beyond complexity.

must have

_____

_____

_____

must avoid

_____

What are your three must-haves and one thing to avoid across the four themes of long life—love, purpose, well-being, and friendship?

PART 4.0

EXPRESSING YOUR LONG LIFE

EXPRESSION

KNOWLEDGE PHILANTHROPY

Expression is giving our design a form.

When I design, expression is a sketch, a model, a prototype, a strategy document, a concept book, a product, a brand, or a system. This book is an expression too.

When we design a life, expression can take the form of a drawing, a poem, or a manifesto. It can be a journey map, or a letter, like the ones on the next pages.

MARSHALL GOLDSMITH IS THE WORLD'S NUMBER ONE LEADERSHIP COACH, BUT EVEN MARSHALL HAS A LIFE COACH—ME! MARSHALL'S EXPRESSION LED TO NOT ONE BUT TWO LEGACY PROJECTS—*100 COACHES* AND HIS *KNOWLEDGE PHILANTHROPY* PROGRAM, BOTH ABOUT GIVING AWAY HIS KNOWLEDGE WITHOUT A FEE.

Michael Bungay Stanier may inspire you to start a new project; Marshall Goldsmith, a new legacy; Cindy Gallop, a new relationship; Lee Kim, a search for making new friends. You might take up a new habit and retrain your body or mind, inspired by Bill Carrier or Z Reitano.

Expression makes our ideas tangible. Our ideas excite us. And when things are exciting, we make time for them. We make a plan, we ask for help, we enlist collaborators. We make them public. We make them happen.

INGREDIENTS OF YOUR LONG LIFE

SUPERPOWER

KRYPTONITE

VALUE

CONSTRAINT

OPPORTUNITY

MAX

CHOICE

EMOTION

NEXT STEP
FOR ME

NEXT STEP FOR
MY COMMUNITY

Marshall's Ingredients

Let's start with the ingredients for the long life you love.

Here are Marshall Goldsmith's ingredients for his Knowledge Philanthropy project—

1. Superpower: Ideas
2. Kryptonite: Prioritizing
3. Value: Making the world better
4. Constraint: Time
5. Opportunity: Building on the existing foundation
6. Choice: Maximum contribution
7. Emotion: Happiness
8. Next Step for Me: Legacy
9. Next Step for Us: Helping each other

NOW ALL YOU NEED TO DO IS REVISIT THE EXERCISES YOU'VE DONE UP UNTIL NOW AND PICK ONE ANSWER FROM EACH THAT EXCITES YOU OR RAISES YOUR TEMPERATURE. THESE ARE ALL THE DESIGN INGREDIENTS YOU WILL USE TO EXPRESS THE LONG LIFE YOU LOVE.

Now it is your turn!

Note: You can also add ingredients from your astronaut metaphor and insights from your metamorphosis. And if there are other influences and inspiration you'd like to include in your design ingredients, feel free to add them here.

JOURNEY MAPS

Most of us grew up with a road map our parents gave us—study hard, go to college, find work, work hard, get married, have children, retire. I am oversimplifying, but you get the idea.

Today, this road map doesn't quite exist, especially not for long life, since these additional years didn't really exist before.

Not having a road map is an incredible challenge, but you now know that challenges are opportunities. The opportunity here is to imagine your original road map. One that truly reflects who we are and what we want and need.

Let's imagine our road maps—with bridges and roads, idea factories and collaboration cafés, dragons to slay, and guardian angels to guide us.

MIST OF THE UNKNOWN

FISH OF GOODLUCK

CARAVANS OF CURIOSITY

OCTOPUS OF CREATIVITY

REEFS OF FEAR OF CHANGE

BRIDGES OF FORGIVENESS

Here are icons and labels to help you get started:

- Bridges and roads that connect things.
- Idea factories, caravans of curiosity, collaboration cafes where things get made.
- Telescopes, ships, compasses to help you find your way.
- Dragons to slay, sharks of self-doubt, reefs of fear that slow you down.
- Guardian angels, fish of luck, treasure of good fortune to speed you up.
- Early discoverers, local people, guides to show you the way.

THESE ILLUSTRATED ICONS COME FROM PARTICIPANTS OF THE DESIGN THE LIFE YOU LOVE VIRTUAL TEA SESSIONS.

SHIPS OF
ADAPTATION
(WHAT TO KEEP,
WHAT TO LEARN)

GODSPEED
(PEOPLE +
THINGS TO
SPEED ME UP)

JOURNAL
OF GRATITUDE

TODAY LAND

BRIDGES OF
DISCOVERY

TELESCOPE
OF "DO I SEE
MYSELF THERE"

A JOURNEY MAP GIVES US A
LAY OF THE LAND, EVEN IF
WE DON'T KNOW ALL THE
DETAILS. IMAGINE YOUR
ROAD MAP—FROM TODAYLAND
TO FUTURELAND.

☀ ☁

LOCAL CLIMATE
(THINGS THAT
AGREE WITH ME)

TRIBES OF
PEOPLE (DO
I SEE MYSELF
AMONG THEM)

FUTURE LAND

TREASURES
(OF OPPORTUNITIES
TO BE FOUND)

🐟

FISH OF
GOOD LUCK
(UNEXPECTED
THINGS OF
GOODNESS)

⭐ ICONS +
SYMBOLS

LETTER

DEAR ME — MY FUTURE SELF,
EMOTION — I AM FEELING SCATTERED, LIKE I AM
FLOUNDERING (IS THAT AN EMOTION?)
SUPERPOWER — I HAVE A GOOD CRITICAL EYE.
I CAN SEE THE BIG PICTURE AND THE DETAIL
SIMULTANEOUSLY. I CHALLENGE THE STATUS
QUO AND QUESTION EXISTING PERCEPTIONS.
CHALLENGE — I AM FINDING IT HARD TO
FIND FOCUS AND CLARITY IN WHAT MOST
EXCITES ME TO PURSUE NEXT.
OPPORTUNITY — MY OPPORTUNITY IS
THAT WE ARE IN A MOMENT OF GREAT
CHANGE, OF WHICH I HOPE TO BE A PART.
VALUE — MY VALUE IS I HAVE A KNACK FOR
SEEING WHAT NEEDS TO CHANGE AND
GETTING CREATIVE ON SOLUTIONS.
INSIGHT — MY HERO IS ME, AND YET
MY PURPOSE IS NOT ABOUT ME.
NEXT STEPS — MY NEXT STEP IS
TO WRITE, SORT, ORGANIZE MY
THOUGHTS AND RESEARCH TO FIND
WHAT REALLY EXCITES ME AND SEE
WHERE IT TAKES ME.
WHAT EXCITES ME — POSITIVE CHANGE
BY CREATING SPACES WHERE COMMUNI-
TIES SUPPORT ONE ANOTHER, VALUE HARD
WORK, AND CONNECT TO A LARGER ECOSYSTEM.
BEAUTY, CRAFT, COMMUNITY, PURPOSE, PEACE.
I HOPE TO SEE YOU WELL + THRIVING IN THE FUTURE.

If your journey map is a visual expression, this letter is your written expression about long life. You can write it in your twenties, and you can write it in your nineties. I have seen both.

You can include your ingredients, top emotion, superpower, kryptonite, value, challenge, opportunity, what excites you, and what excited you for your community in the form of a letter.

Deciding who the letter is addressed to is up to you—your future self, your kids, or your partner, your hero. You pick!

VERDA ALEXANDER IS THE COFOUNDER, ARTIST IN RESIDENCE, AND ACTIVIST OF THE AWARD-WINNING STUDIO O+A, FAMOUS FOR THE OFFICES THEY HAVE DESIGNED FOR FACEBOOK, UBER, MICROSOFT, AND OTHERS. HERE IS HER LETTER TO HER FUTURE SELF.

The first draft, the first couple of sketches, and the first mock-up are about getting the idea out of your head. Give yourself no more than ten minutes to write your first draft. Go with your gut, and don't worry about making it perfect.

As my mentor Bruce Hannah, award-winning designer and teacher to some of the best designers in the world, would tell us, "Mock it up before you fock it up."

189

PART 5.0

LIVING YOUR LONG LIFE

THE USER
IN YOU

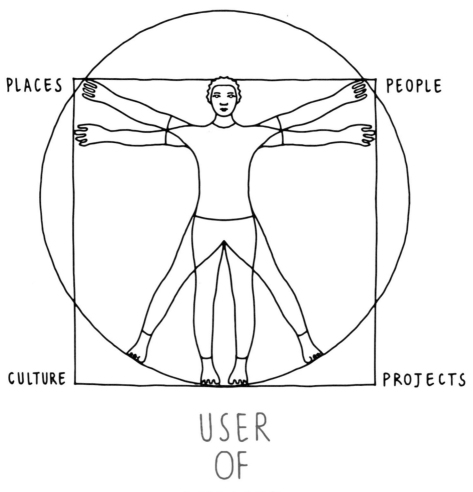

PLACES

PEOPLE

CULTURE

PROJECTS

USER
OF
MY LIFE

Congratulations! You've designed the long life you love.

Here are a few things I recommend to help you bring your design ideas to life:

- Remember, the user of this life is you. Have empathy for yourself.

- Get your ideas out of your head and onto paper to see them. Draw, write, map them out.

- Design is a collaboration. Enlist collaborators in your designs (more on this on page 194.)

- Design is an iterative cycle. Start small, test your idea, learn, refine, and test again.

HELP ME
HELP YOU

Designing is collaborating. You need collaborators to look at the same problem from different angles, to build on each other's ideas, and for deep learning and generous creativity. Asking for help is inherent in good design.

So, what is one thing you need help with as you design your long life?

Instead of answering it yourself, which is harder to do, collaborate with your friends and ask them to give you ideas. Note their answers and thank them—even if you've heard or tried their ideas before, or even if you don't like their ideas, thank them.

Remember, when you ask for help, you are also opening the door for the other person to do the same.

This exercise is inspired by Marshall Goldsmith.

AS YOU DESIGN YOUR LONG
LIFE, WHAT IS ONE THING
YOU NEED HELP WITH?

LONG LIFE

oxo peeler   this book

This book could've been a book about aging. But it's not. What makes this book unique is even though it's inspired by the wisdom of older people, anyone can use it at any age. This book is the OXO Good Grips of books. Let me explain.

OXO Good Grips potato peeler is one of the legends of design. It's even in my first book, *Design the Life You Love*. The peeler was originally designed for older people with arthritis, but it became a product loved by everyone, universally, because its soft, pliable handle is comfortable for anyone, regardless of their age. We probably all have a Good Grips peeler in our homes.

This book is the equivalent of Good Grips for life design. It's informed by the wisdom and knowledge of older people, but the lessons, humor, and insights they offer will serve all of us. That is what makes this book unique.

Thank you for reading it!

IT IS NEVER TOO LATE OR TOO EARLY TO DESIGN YOUR LONG LIFE!

PART 6.0

INSPIRATION

THINGS THAT HAVE INSPIRED ME

Every designer needs inspiration. Inspiration shows us parts of the solution in different, disparate places. And seeing those parts gives us the optimism that there's a solution to be found. They excite us and give us the creative energy to move forward with hope.

Here's an incomplete list of people, books, articles, podcasts, and blogs that inspired me as I was researching, drawing, and writing this book. Every day I would read or listen to something new that excited me. There must be so much more.

I can just hear you say, "You didn't read this or listen to this, Ayse!" Let me know your favorites, as I am still a beginner.

Let's start with our research with The Scan Foundation (thescanfoundation.org), which is available online:

Codesigning with Older People Report and Codesign Kit & Facilitator's Guide

And visit Alive Ventures at *aliveventures.co*, the venture studio John Zapolski founded, for how designers, entrepreneurs, and older people are coming together to solve for a more joyful, longer life. In total transparency, we designed the Alive brand.

BOOKS

THE 100-YEAR LIFE. LYNDA GRATTON, ANDREW SCOTT

BY DESIGN. RALPH CAPLAN

THE CREATIVE HABIT. BY TWYLA THARP AND MARK REITER

THE DESIGN OF EVERYDAY THINGS. BY DON NORMAN

THE EARNED LIFE. BY MARSHALL GOLDSMITH AND MARK REITER

THE FREEDOM OF CONSTRAINTS. BY DARCY VERHUN

THE HAPPINESS HYPOTHESIS. BY JONATHAN HAIDT

NO TIME TO SPARE. URSULA LE GUIN

TO BE HONEST. BY RON CARUCCI

TRIGGERS. BY MARSHALL GOLDSMITH AND MARK REITER

VISUALEADERSHIP. BY TODD CHERCHES

WISDOM AT WORK. BY CHIP CONLEY

ARTICLES

"MY FATHER ADDRESSES ME ON THE FACTS OF OLD AGE"

BY GRACE PALEY, *THE NEW YORKER*

"I WROTE THE BOOK ON USER-FRIENDLY DESIGN. WHAT I SEE TODAY HORRIFIES ME"

BY DON NORMAN, FAST COMPANY

"WHY START ROMAN"

BY ZACHARIAH REITANO, MEDIUM

"WHY SLEEPING WITH YOUNGER MEN IS BEST—NO MATTER HOW OLD YOU ARE"

BY CINDY GALLOP, THE CUT, *NEW YORK MAGAZINE*

"'WEARABLE TRACY' AND CONNECTIONS FORGED THROUGH FUNKY HATS"

BY RACHEL SYME, *THE NEW YORKER*

"32 EASY EXERCISES TO BOOST YOUR CREATIVITY EVERY DAY"

BY AYSE BIRSEL, INC.COM

PODCASTS

HIDDEN BRAIN: BEING KIND TO YOURSELF

HIDDEN BRAIN: LAUGHTER: THE BEST MEDICINE

INNOVATION HUB: WHEN ROMANCE MEETS RATIOS

DESIGN MATTERS WITH DEBBIE MILLMAN: CINDY GALLOP

TEDx TALKS

RETHINKING AGING: MENTORING A NEW GENERATION. **BY DEBBIE HEISER**

THE ART OF BEING YOURSELF. **BY CAROLINE MCHUGH**

ACKNOWLEDGMENTS

My family, Bibi, Awa, Alev, Waly—may you live very, very long lives you love.

My elders, my parents, Özgül + Mahmut Birsel; my other parents, Gisele + Mamadou Seck; my aunts and uncles, Alev Bilgen, Ayse + Ismet Birsel, Sezer + Üner Birkan, Esin + Gün Birsel; my great uncle, Münir Birsel; my grandparents, Zerrin + Emin Birsel; my 2nd family, Ralph Caplan, Christine Downton and Rowena Reed—this book is a love letter to you.

My friends, Leah Caplan, my creative doula who helps me birth my ideas, including this book; Seda Evis and Meltem Parlak, my collaborators—it's a privilege to work on things we love together.

My clients, Ana Pinto da Silva, Bruce Chernof, John Zapolski, and the extraordinary participants who came to our co-design workshops—thank you for pioneering this work.

My champions, Marshall Goldsmith, Beth Polish, Scott Osman, Mark Reiter, Dawn Barber, Chester Elton, Sanyin Siang, Julie + Bill Carrier—my life is better because of you.

My agent, Meg Thompson—we did it again.

My book collaborators, Shannon Fabricant and Frances Soo Ping Chow at Running Press, and Lee Iley, at Lee Iley Design—thank you for bringing this book to life with conviction and beauty.

My Virtual Tea community, AKA, people of AuthentiCity— you cheered me to the finish line.

Ayse (pronounced Eye-Shay) Birsel is one of the world's leading industrial designers. She has designed hundreds of products, from toilet seats to office systems to potato peelers to concept cars. You've probably held, sat on, or worked in something she has designed for Herman Miller "Knoll," Target, or Toyota, among many others. Her work has earned her several nicknames—Queen of Toilets, Queen Bee (for offices), and Design Evangelista. *Interior Design* magazine awarded her Best of Year Product Designer of 2020. She is one of the Most Creative People In Business, according to Fast Company. She was shortlisted among the world's top 8 coaches by Thinkers50 for Marshall Goldsmith Distinguished Achievement Award for Coaching and Mentoring. She is the author of *Design the Life You Love* and is recognized as "The #1 Coach for Life Design." Her design process, Deconstruction:Reconstruction™, is the red thread across all her work, including this book. Her work can be found in the permanent collection of the Museum of Modern Art (MoMA). Ayse was born in Turkey and came to New York City, where she now lives and works, with a Fulbright scholarship.

This book was designed for everyone, with an age and different-ability friendly layout.

We used Raleway sans-serif font in 14 point size for the main text, since 12 to 14 point sans-serif font is said to be best for easy readability.

In my drawings, we opted for capital lettering and minimized my cursive handwriting.

For titles we used demi-bold to make the blue-colored titles stand out. For the blue accent color, we looked for a hue that was bright enough to be visually vibrant but with enough contrast to be legible.

We left lots of white space to relax the eye and, at the same time, make it easier to focus on what you are reading.

Design is inherently visual, and because of this, I drew the ideas in this book as much as I wrote about them.

Illustrations: Ayse Birsel
Book and Cover Design: Lee Iley
Creative Advisor: Leah Caplan
Creative Director: Frances Soo Ping Chow

RUNNING PRESS

HACHETTE BOOK GROUP

1290 AVENUE OF THE AMERICAS, NEW YORK, NY 10104

WWW.RUNNINGPRESS.COM

@RUNNING_PRESS

PRINTED IN ITALY

FIRST EDITION: DECEMBER 2022

PUBLISHED BY RUNNING PRESS, AN IMPRINT OF PERSEUS BOOKS, LLC,
A SUBSIDIARY OF HACHETTE BOOK GROUP, INC. THE RUNNING PRESS
NAME AND LOGO ARE TRADEMARKS OF THE HACHETTE BOOK GROUP.

THE HACHETTE SPEAKERS BUREAU PROVIDES A WIDE RANGE OF
AUTHORS FOR SPEAKING EVENTS. TO FIND OUT MORE, GO TO
WWW.HACHETTESPEAKERSBUREAU.COM OR CALL (866) 376-6591.
THE PUBLISHER IS NOT RESPONSIBLE FOR WEBSITES (OR THEIR CONTENT)
THAT ARE NOT OWNED BY THE PUBLISHER.

ISBNS: 978-0-7624-8115-6 (HARDCOVER), 978-0-7624-8116-3 (EBOOK)

LIBRARY OF CONGRESS CONTROL NUMBER: 2022937066

ELCO

10 9 8 7 6 5 4 3 2 1

THE E
THE
BEGIN